MORE PRAISE FOR *FIRES IN THE MIND*

"A unique approach to exploring the question of how teachers can better engage and inspire today's students." —Anthony Rebora, *Education Week/Teacher*

"A relief and a wakeup call to anyone who worries about the apathy of today's youth." — Daniel Greene, *Education Review*

"This inspiring book helps us understand that all students have intrinsic motivation and ability. Cushman's stories and examples show us how to find and unlock that capacity and help students accomplish more than they—or we—thought possible." —Ben Levin, author, *How to Change 5000 Schools*

"A wonderful book for both practitioners and policymakers. Students talk about how they practice getting better at things they love to do, applying their learning to make school more sensible, meaningful, and productive for them and their teachers." —Elliot Washor, co-director, Big Picture Learning

"No matter what stage we're at as educators, every teacher can mine this book for many helpful nuggets to support student mastery. We can help ignite 'fires in the minds' of our kids, and this wonderful book makes an excellent fire starter." —Teacher Leaders Network, Center for Teaching Quality, Los Angeles Unified School District

"If you are looking for a book that is inspiring and motivating, this is the one. This is educational reform within the four walls of your classroom!" —Megan Palevich, *Good Reads*

"Depicts kids—all kinds of kids—as deeply passionate and self-propelled learners, who don't need adults driving them to get started, to get interested. They figure out how to be good, because they are profoundly engaged in wanting to know something." —Kirsten Olsen, author, *Wounded by School*

"Offers a unique window into what all educators ought to consider as vastly important: igniting the passion for learning inherent in us all." —Ronald J. Newell, author, *Passion for Learning*

"Should be studied by teachers and used as a model for eliciting the many fires in the minds of their students. What better way to learn how to transform our practices?" —Bena Kallick, author, *Learning and Leading with Habits of Mind*

"As a nation we need to return our educational focus to true scholarship—beyond test scores, we need to support students to strive for excellence in their academic, artistic, and civic work. In this volume Kathleen Cushman brings her celebrated collection of student voices to this crucial issue." —Ron Berger, Expeditionary Learning Schools, and author, *An Ethic of Excellence*

"A wonderful book that gave me lots of new insights about what motivates and inspires young minds." —Michael Klonsky, director, Small Schools Workshop (in *Catalyst Caucus*)

"I love the book because it makes sense. If my students start this thinking in the fall, they will be able to draw on it when they actually do get into student teaching." —Shari Saunders, teacher educator, University of Michigan Graduate School of Education

"A highly readable book for teens, parents, teachers, administrators, community members, and maybe even those politicians and billionaire business people who think they should be the ones deciding how to improve education in our nation. The prescription here is decidedly different from just firing all us lazy, bad teachers." —*Action Reader blog, "What She Read"*

PRAISE FOR KATHLEEN CUSHMAN'S BOOKS WITH STUDENTS

When kids are finally given a voice, it's always amazing to me how on target their perceptions of schools are! —Bob Mackin, Director, America's Choice High Schools

Fires in the Bathroom tells it like it is. . . . All educators should read this book. Parents too. There is much wisdom here. —Linda Darling-Hammond, Stanford University

Wonderful and painful to read. . . . *Fires in the Bathroom* gives me so many ideas about what we could do differently tomorrow. —Deborah Meier, author, *The Power of Their Ideas*

The minds of students seem so mysterious to most adults. *Fires in the Middle School Bathroom* lets the students tell their own stories in their own voices. The book sheds welcome new light on what middle school students really care about and how they experience their days in school. —William Damon, Director, Stanford Center on Adolescence

Sent to the Principal **should be read by every high school principal in the country.** The book eloquently uses the words of students in a powerful way that no one can ignore. It will provide tremendous grist for the important conversations that need to take place to transform our high schools. — Joseph DiMartino, Education Alliance, Brown University

Through the ears, eyes, voices, tastes, and hands of students, *Sent to the Principal* gives us student insights that are frank, honest, simply delivered, and valuable for changing schools. —Elliot Washor, Ed.D., Co-director, Big Picture Company

I couldn't put this book down. *Sent to the Principal* gently leads the school leader to change his or her personal style of leading, but also encourages institutionalized responses. —Robert McCarthy, thirty-year principal and mentor, Colorado Small Schools Initiative

Parents, teachers, and just plain adults would do well to listen to the young men and women in *What We Can't Tell You,* if the creation of a truly humane society is still our goal. —Thomas J. Cottle, author of *Mind Fields: Adolescent Consciousness in a Culture of Distraction,* professor of education, Boston University

*This book is dedicated
to all the students waiting to catch fire
and all the teachers
who notice and cherish the sparks*

Fires in the Mind

What Kids Can Tell Us
About Motivation and Mastery

Kathleen Cushman

and the students of What Kids Can Do

JOSSEY-BASS
A Wiley Imprint
www.josseybass.com

Published by Jossey-Bass
A Wiley Imprint
989 Market Street, San Francisco, CA 94103-1741—www.josseybass.com

Jossey-Bass books and products are available through most bookstores. To contact Jossey-Bass directly call our Customer Care Department within the U.S. at 800-956-7739, outside the U.S. at 317-572-3986, or fax 317-572-4002.

Jossey-Bass also publishes its books in a variety of electronic formats. Some content that appears in print may not be available in electronic books.

Type design by Sandra Delany.

Library of Congress Cataloging-in-Publication Data

Cushman, Kathleen.
Fires in the mind : what kids can tell us about motivation and mastery / Kathleen Cushman.
    p. cm.
  Includes bibliographical references and index.
  ISBN 978-0-470-64603-8 (hardcover); 978-1-118-16021-3 (paper); 978-0-470-64950-3 (ebk.); 978-0-470-64949-7 (ebk.); 978-0-470-64947-3 (ebk.)
  1. Mastery learning. 2. Motivation in education. 3. Teenagers—Education. I. Title.
LB1031.4.C87 2010
370.15'4—dc22
                                2010013840

Printed in the United States of America.
FIRST EDITION
HB Printing   10 9 8 7 6 5 4 3 2
PB Printing   10 9 8 7 6 5 4 3 2 1

Contents

Foreword

ASKING STUDENTS TO TALK ABOUT their education is so simple that—whether we are teachers, parents, researchers, or policymakers—we inevitably forget to do it. Yet when we do invite them to the table with adults, the youth in our classrooms and communities will shed surprising new light on our most intransigent educational dilemmas. What makes young people catch fire, work hard, and persist despite difficulties? What supports and structures do they need in order to thrive and contribute, in both school and society?

Those are the questions that this book addresses, and for over a quarter-century at MetLife and MetLife Foundation, we have put the same questions at the center of our work with education. The *Metlife Survey of the American Teacher*—which each year gathers the views of a broad and representative sample of those closest to the classroom—teachers, principals, parents, students—consistently highlights the beliefs, practices, and experiences of young people as well as their teachers. As *Fires in the Mind* goes to press, MetLife is just releasing our twenty-sixth such report, based on our 2009 survey and titled "Collaborating for Student Success." Its findings go to the heart of the issues raised here by the students of What Kids Can Do.

Merely asking young people about their learning will not by itself foster their ambitious goals and high expectations, their motivation and mastery. We need also to listen closely, and to collaborate with youth on analyzing the disparities between their experiences and what their elders report.

Four out of five teachers and principals in our 2009 survey told us that they believe connecting classroom instruction to the real world would have a major impact on student achievement. They also held that addressing the individual needs of diverse students is necessary to student success. A school culture where students feel responsible and accountable for their own education, they said, would greatly affect student achievement.

In that same survey, however, a majority of students reported that their teachers very rarely—or never—speak to them personally about things that matter to the students. Over a quarter of secondary school students said their teachers do not connect the school curriculum to its applications in the outside world. And only one in four students felt strongly that school let them use their abilities and their creativity.

What should we conclude from such disparate perspectives? In *Fires in the Mind,* What Kids Can Do asks us to join young people in investigating the answers. Students here recount the conditions that ignite their curiosity and inspire them to strive for excellence, in very different contexts including school, home, and community. They point out which practices successfully coach them through the necessary hardships of learning, and which sap their desire to keep up the struggle. They interview adults who have attained mastery in their fields, and analyze the habits that got them to that point. They consider the cognitive research about developing expertise, and then they look at various school experiences, such as homework, through that lens.

The students' voices in this book start a vital conversation about "what it takes to get really good at something." For all our young people to develop to their full potential, that conversation must now continue among adults and youth in our schools, homes, and communities. I urge each reader to contribute your perspective, your voice, and the rich details of your experiences to the dialogue ahead. As we construct a common understanding among youth and adults, we will also be developing mastery for the future we are shaping every day.

Dennis White
President and CEO, MetLife Foundation

Fires in the Mind

CHAPTER ONE

What Does It Take to Get Good?

I N A BIG PUBLIC HIGH SCHOOL on the west side of Chicago, a ninth-grade boy named Joshua is describing the thing he does best in life. We sit in his reading and writing classroom, twenty-eight students in a circle, me with an audio recorder. "I'm real good at architecture," Joshua says matter-of-factly.

> **WHAT KIDS TELL US**
>
> **Everything takes practice. It's not like one day you can just get up and say, "I'm going to do something." You got to practice at it.**
>
> **– DARRIUS**

I am startled, even skeptical. Architecture in ninth grade? How?

Joshua goes on. His interest started when he was about eleven, he says, as he watched his uncle, a building contractor, draw up plans on a computer.

> I was, like, "Can I do it?" And once I tried it, I liked it. I can draw out the layout of a building, make electrical wires in the layout, stuff like that. It was hard learning how to use the software, because it was something I'd never used before. It took me a couple months—it was real frustrating. I remember trying to find out how to make a wall longer, and my uncle, he wasn't there to help me. I had to go to "Help" to read how to do it. I don't like reading, but I was determined to learn how to use this software.
>
> – JOSHUA F.

All of us in the room believe him now, because Joshua is talking about a situation most of us know well: trying to master something hard. We recognize his frustration as he goes after what he wants that is just beyond his reach. We hear how his resolve and confidence increase as he pushes past obstacles. And when Joshua tells us the result, we hear his pride and purpose. Last summer one of his neighbors was planning to put up a small strip mall nearby. The neighbor couldn't afford to pay a designer, so he asked Joshua—a reluctant reader who was just about to enter ninth grade—to draw up the plans.

THE PRACTICE PROJECT

What does it take, I asked the students speaking with me that day, to get *really good* at something?

A simple question, it reverberates at many levels. It matters equally to youth and adults, rich and poor, professional, artist, and tradesperson. Its answers have the potential to transform our schools and communities. And exciting research on the question of developing expertise has emerged in recent decades from the field of cognitive psychology.

Powerful new evidence shows that opportunity and practice have far more impact on high performance than does innate talent. We all have heard by now that *ten thousand hours* of practice—that's three hours a day, six days a week, for ten years—goes into making someone an expert.

To understand what this means for everyday teaching and learning, I asked adolescents themselves in an initiative sponsored by the national nonprofit What Kids Can Do. Reaching out to schools and youth organizations, I looked not for prodigies but for ordinary teenagers willing to talk with me about their lives and learning. The net we cast drew in 160 students from diverse backgrounds around the United States, ranging from cities to rural communities. Together we explored how young people acquire the knowledge, skills, and habits that help them rise to mastery in a field.

To my surprise, every one of these youth could name something they were already good at. Many of them—not just the unusually talented—were even growing expert at it, although sometimes the adults in their lives had not noticed. Their examples kept coming: music, dance, drawing, drama, knitting, chess, video games, running, soccer, building robots, braiding hair, writing poems, skateboarding, cooking. So much sustained practice in pursuit of mastery—and so much of it happening outside of school!

In days of discussion, the kids and I picked apart how they got started at these activities, why they kept going, and what setbacks and satisfactions they experienced as they put in the necessary practice. We discovered a great deal about why young people engage deeply in work that challenges them. And as we analyzed their experiences, we also began to think differently about what goes on in schools. Could what these young people already understood about practice also apply to their academic learning? Could teachers build on kids' strengths and affinities, coaching them in the same habits that experts use? What did it take to light a fire in the mind of an adolescent that would fuel a lifelong passion for learning?

STARTING OUT AND KEEPING GOING

These teenagers' stories brought into vivid relief the research on how expertise develops. Few of them started their chosen activity because they had "natural talent." Largely, they gravitated to something because it looked like fun, because they wanted to be with others who were doing it, and because someone gave them a chance and encouraged them.

Chapter Two, "Catching the Spark," is filled with their stories of how they caught that first spark. Joey, a nationally ranked archer at sixteen, first picked up a bow and arrow at six, because he wanted to "hang out with my dad in the backyard and shoot bales." Ninoshka learned to knit from her grandmother, who "would not be mad at me, no matter what came out wrong, because she was trying to make me better at it." Kellie tried Double Dutch jump rope only when her big sister counted her down to the first scary move.

Kids have to want something before they risk trying, said Ariel, a young skateboarder in New York City.

> If something's very fun-looking to you, you just get right into it. That inspiration from watching other people do new things, it gives you the confidence in yourself where you can go out and try it. — ARIEL V.

Even a small success at the start helped their initial interest burn bright, these young people said. Not far into their learning, however, they faced significant frustration—and what happened next made a critical difference. To succeed, they would have to stick with it, as they tell us in Chapter Three, "Keeping at It."

"Everything takes practice," said Darrius, a Chicago student bent on becoming an artist.

> It's not like one day you can just get up and say, "I'm going to do something." You got to practice at it. You might be good at it when you first start off, but you still got to practice so you can get better, because no one's perfect. Like me: I can draw real good. But certain things that I want to do in drawing I can't do right now. So I just keep working at it. — DARRIUS

When they hit discouraging points, most students said, they continued only if they had a strong relationship with someone who supported them through the rough spots. "The people who sit next to you have a big part in how you get better at something," observed Janiy, who studied piano.

> Without them you can start getting lazy, and you want to give up if you don't get it right the first time. I give up on the inside, and she tells me, "Again. Come on—once more." – JANIY

In school too these youth persisted with challenging material only when their practice was supported. From their outside activities they had gained a healthy respect for the base of knowledge they needed in order to do something well. They knew that the right kind of practice would help them recall what they had learned, just when they needed it later.

Mike, a young drummer from Maine, told of learning the double-stroke roll, "where your stick bounces once on the snare, like 'buh-*bum*,' and you hit the other stick and it bounces." His teacher kept him practicing it for weeks, until the action came to him effortlessly.

> You just have to go slow, and play that forever until you understand the movement. Then once you get comfortable with it, you just work your way up, play a little bit faster, and then just a little bit faster. – MIKE

The wrong kind of practice, however, could stop these young learners in their tracks. If she couldn't expect to succeed at something with a reasonable amount of effort, Iona said, she wouldn't even bother to try.

> When people are only faced with their failures, they tend to want to give up. They need help to see their own progress, so that they don't only see how bad they are doing. They need to see the fun in it, and to see some reward in completing the task. – IONA

These teenagers were describing what cognitive researchers such as K. Anders Ericsson call *deliberate practice*. Their learning tasks were set at a challenge level just right for them. They repeated a task in a focused, attentive way, at intervals that helped them recall its key elements. All along they received and adjusted to feedback, correcting their mistakes and savoring small successes. (In Chapter Five, "Exploring Deliberate Practice," they explore the elements of deliberate practice in their most compelling activities.)

When their practice went just right, kids told me, they felt caught up in a state of "flow": the energized, full involvement of going after a challenge within their reach. As Aaron, a basketball player, described it:

> Running down the court, it's like a lion hunting for its prey: there's nothing else on its mind but that prey. And that's what makes it so beautiful, just the strive of it. — AARON S.

LEARNING FROM EXPERTS

Watching accomplished people do something well often made these teenagers want to practice even more. Talking to experts in person was even better. As Mike said, "If I meet a musician I look up to, everything he says is like it was bolded out."

So I sent students out to interview people from their communities whom they considered masters in their fields—plumbers, farmers, physicians, church organists, psychologists, engineers, and so on. And as the kids transcribed those interviews, they saw many similarities to their own learning journeys.

Every expert's story started with a spark of interest that somebody noticed and fanned. All had the opportunity to explore that interest further, with someone nearby to encourage, critique, and suggest next steps. Small successes along the way rewarded hours of practice—and with a challenge met, the experts wanted to go further.

Whether the person interviewed was a surgeon, a tattoo artist, or a detective, each of these experts had developed certain habits along the way. Some were ways of thinking, we realized, and others were ways of approaching their work. The students and I made a list and returned to it often, checking whether the kids were developing these same habits through their own practice. (We say more about this in Chapter Four, "Asking the Experts.")

Was it competition or collaboration, public performance or private satisfactions that drove these experts through their years of practice? These are among the questions that my students address in Chapter Six, "Practice and Performance." But in all the answers they gathered, they recognized the quality of flow—"the strive of it"—that they already knew well. Energized by that discovery, the kids were ready to explore what could bring that full engagement into schoolwork.

TAKING PRACTICE TO SCHOOL

Nothing compared to "the strive of it," these young people agreed. Yet they felt that sense of involvement in a challenge most fully outside of the classroom. Some kids threw themselves into reading, writing, and the arts, but even those activities rarely coincided with their formal schooling. How might schools transfer the excitement of learning from one realm to the other? As one student observed,

> If teachers knew what gave us that driving force to do better, they could apply that, so that everyone can do things to the best of their ability. — AVELINA

Our Practice Project was already sharpening these young people's curiosity about learning, giving them a new way to talk about it and turning them into "experts in expertise." Perhaps their teachers too could gain new insights from looking closely at out-of-school learning. Such understanding could have only good effects, said Rachel, a San Antonio student.

> The teachers you have along the way can either make or break you. They pass along to you their own learning process. – RACHEL M.

In Chapter Seven, "Bringing Practice into the Classroom," the students do not suggest making direct links between their interests and school subjects. Instead, they remind teachers of the meaning and value they have found in outside-school commitments, and ask them to look for that in school subjects, too. As Micah, in San Antonio, explained:

> You want to delve into the reason why you are doing something, instead of just blindly following what the teacher tells you to do. If you are getting the answer without really realizing why it's important, it's empty. You are not really learning. You are going to drop that later, because it has no importance to you in your life. – MICAH

Sometimes, Samantha said, teachers seemed to focus more on students' standardized test results than on their actual understanding.

> They go too much by the book. They worry about the perfect answer, rather than worrying about if we've learned something. – SAMANTHA

Homework too came under their scrutiny. In Chapter Eight, "Is Homework Deliberate Practice?" the students hold up their assignments to the criteria for deliberate practice and find them largely wanting. Often homework has little to do with what individual students need to practice, and they respond by giving it little of their attention.

Their best work at school, these teenagers said, got them to practice the *habits* we had seen our experts using—adapting the details to fit each learner's profile. Darrian, for example, joined her school's chess club in elementary school and, a few years later, learned to like math as well.

> Actually, math is my favorite subject now. I like figuring out how to do problems, and I find logic questions so much fun. I think chess helped me find that deep inside—it was probably always there, but I just never knew where it was. – DARRIAN

For other students, the most compelling school experiences involved hands-on projects in which they could work in teams toward an outcome that mattered to them. (We devote Chapter Nine, "School Projects That Build Expert Habits," to this subject.) Tyler described a science project involving genetic research and technology that had gripped his imagination for months.

> One driving factor here is the experiment itself: the curiosity about what the answer will be! Another is the real-world application: being able to develop something that can actually help people. – TYLER

TEN THOUSAND HOURS

What can we draw from teenagers' outside-school experiences to inform what—and how—we ask them to practice in school? How would our classroom teaching change, if we used expert habits as our touchstone? What part would parents and other adults outside of the school play in the education of adolescents?

As we listen in coming chapters to young people describe their most compelling pursuits, we will learn more about how the right conditions can motivate youth to practice until they reach mastery. And a picture will emerge of a shared community of knowledge-building that embraces home, classroom, and outside learning opportunities.

In our concluding chapter, Chapter Ten, "Making School a Community of Practice," students offer concrete suggestions for helping schools function more like expert learning situations outside of the classroom. When youth are willing to help think through that shift with adults, as they do here, a powerful learning partnership can result. (In Appendix A we outline a five-day curriculum for groups that want to try it.) Even more important, as students come to recognize that all teaching is also a practice, they join an expert culture that intertwines their learning with teachers' own.

> To break down concepts and make them understandable is an art. And to relate to students and tailor your teaching style to all different types of learners is a sort of expertise. – BRIDGET

When adults openly explore genuine questions about getting to mastery—and include young people's knowledge and experiences in that exploration—we model the expert's habit of taking intellectual and creative risks. We demonstrate that we too always have things we need to understand better, and things we need to practice. We teach kids to approach any lack of understanding as a puzzle: stretching the limits of their competence, continually testing new possibilities, and seeing how they work out. As they expand their knowledge and skills, young people, like us, will discover even more challenging puzzles they want to tackle—not just outside of school but as part of it.

"Train every day, then you will see," advised the samurai Musashi four hundred years ago. Ten thousand hours—that roughly corresponds to the time students spend in school during four years of high school and four years of college. What are we asking our youth to practice in that precious time? What fires are we lighting in their minds?

CHAPTER TWO

Catching the Spark

WHEN KASIA WAS a four-year-old in Harlem, her mother came home from the store with a bright-colored activity book to keep her busy during school vacation week. It turned out to be a second-grade math workbook, but it looked like fun, so Kasia took it over to her grandmother's place, where her older cousins got her started on it. She spent the whole week figuring out how numbers work, and her family treated her like a star every time she worked out another problem.

> ## WHAT KIDS TELL US
>
> **For once in my life I didn't have anyone forcing me to do something. I didn't have a motive, beyond that of having fun. I just wanted to experience and possibly learn something new. It was shocking how much fun I had at something I had never done before.**
>
> — BERENICE

Kasia grew up thinking of math as her special talent. Now in tenth grade, she still loves figuring out problems and helping other students with theirs.

> Math all round is not easy, but imperfection is what makes your strive for perfection better. If my friends are having trouble, I encourage them to continue what they are doing, for you learn from mistakes and your experience. – KASIA

We often jump to the conclusion that students' aptitudes arrived with them at birth and have been developing ever since. But stories like Kasia's give a more complicated picture.

A young person's natural strengths, family setting, cultural contexts, and social ties all may contribute to his or her taking the first steps toward developing a particular skill. In one family, almost everybody might play music; in another, sports may dominate. A rural community may bring up its youth to participate in a central economic activity such as farming, fishing, or ski tourism. A group of friends may gravitate to puzzles or computer games. A school may have a popular chess program or debating team. A neighborhood youth center might offer lessons in swimming, dance, or martial arts.

In fact, my students mostly said that they took up an activity simply because it gave them pleasure to join others in something enjoyable. To feel that satisfaction, they took whatever opportunities they had: at home, at play, in school, or out in their community.

Seldom, however, did my young collaborators develop a compelling interest without someone else's involvement. More important than a natural inclination or a chance to share some fun, their stories show, was the person who (often quite literally) could take them to where they wanted and needed to go.

With that support, step by step, they acquired new confidence that they could come to do something well. And as they had the chance to try out authentic tasks at a level just beyond their competence, their interest and confidence grew.

Most of this book's accounts of how students came to excel do not emphasize inborn talent—a disposition, either neurological or temperamental, toward tinkering with things mechanical or making music or art. Instead, they are stories of interest and skill built on opportunity and relationships. In this chapter, my student collaborators tell of their beginnings. "What do you remember," I asked them, "about getting started at what you do well? Where were you, and how did it happen?"

GENERATIONS PASSING SKILLS DOWN

As a child, Odell idolized his older cousin, a teenager who taught him to write when Odell was five and who died a few years later.

> He's the one that taught me how to really express myself. He would talk to me in slang and I didn't know what he was saying. I would have to write it down, and he told me how to write in different ways, to say what you want to mean. — ODELL

Odell remembers riding on the subway with his mother just after his cousin's death, writing on a pad of paper the words that filled his head.

> I wrote about how noisy it was, but it wasn't like it was annoying— it was just how I felt. I wrote it like it was a puzzle getting put together. My mom was covering her ears, but I was realizing this is a *true world*, you know what I mean? — ODELL

That impulse to make art from his experience drove Odell to write poetry every chance he got. His mother loved to listen to his work, and he always trusted her opinions about it. Through the years she often took him to performances at poetry clubs. Now that he is in high school in Long Beach, California, Odell writes more than twenty poems a day and considers himself above all a poet. "I'd like to spark the brain that will change the world by my writing," he said.

> I'm thinking, and which word to write just snaps into me. It just flows into my brain and then I outlet it through when I write. There is no blocking me. I could do it in the most loudest rooms. It turns my head into a quiet place. It's refreshing, like drinking something cold on a warm day. — ODELL

Odell is just one of my student collaborators who found a passion for something passed down to them by older family members. In San Antonio, for example, Ruben grew up working on an old "muscle car" that his father, a car mechanic, kept around.

> When my dad was taking his old engine out of his Cutlass and putting a bigger one in so he could go faster, pretty much since that time I have always wanted that kind of car and that kind of engine. Starting when I was about eleven, I would change the oil, change spark plugs, change the brakes on that car. I got my permit at fifteen, but my dad had taught me how to drive standard on his truck when I was twelve. – RUBEN

When Keila was growing up in New York City, her grandmother always designed and sewed her clothes. Keila was often at the older woman's side as she made a first communion dress or transformed an aunt's cast-off outfit into a Halloween costume that fit the young girl perfectly.

> I loved to watch her sew, and I wanted to learn so I could make the clothes I liked. After school I sat next to her and she showed me how to use the sewing machine and how to use patterns with fabric. Then she would let me try. It was hard because my grandmother's English is not very good and I didn't speak a lot of Spanish. And I grew frustrated when the talent did not instantly come to me. – KEILA

It did not take long, however, before Keila was sketching out patterns of her own. She knew she was getting good when she first planned out and made her own costume for Halloween. "I could actually wear it outside," she said, "and it looked like a store-bought dress!"

Whatever the consuming passion of their significant elders, young people are often taking it in somehow. In the small Maine town where Kenzie grew up, his dad was "big into soccer." He first got his son out on the field at the age of four or five, and with his father's encouragement, Kenzie's own interest slowly grew.

> At first I had absolutely no sense of what I had to do. I was just running around. I slowly learned the very basics—that gave me some concept of what I was doing, and made me care about the game a little bit more. It took a couple of years, playing fourteen or sixteen weeks a year, till I got really fluent and comfortable. Then over the years I developed a passion for soccer, and a knack for it.
> — KENZIE

From the age of three or four Tyler loved to do scientific experiments with his grandfather. "He would explain to me how glow-in-the-dark things work on an atomic level, as if I wasn't a little kid," he said. "And I actually understood what he was talking about. I remember in third grade trying to explain it to my class."

By Tyler's high school years in San Diego, his grandfather's passion for how things worked had become his own. "In school I'm extremely disorganized," he said. "I'm not book smart." Outside of school, however, he spent most of his free time building things that he engineered himself. Using materials he had scrounged and scraped together, he built a catapult in his back yard, then went on to make his own skateboard.

> I tried to educate myself and figure it out, engineer it down to the level where I could complete it. I worked on it for four months. Being able to commit myself to completing a task, it's a powerful experience. — TYLER

Simply by spending time with an older person they looked up to, Tyler and these other students experienced the contagious excitement of training one's mind on a challenge. What was passed down the generations did include important skills and knowledge. But at least as important was that the younger people caught a vital sense that the activity held high value—so they wanted to do it too.

FUN, COMPANIONSHIP, CHALLENGE

Many of my young collaborators got interested in a field because of the sheer pleasure of fooling around with something fun to do. Berenice remembers the freedom she felt on a school retreat at a camp in the countryside, when she decided to try canoeing for the first time.

> Being able to make my own decision made it more free. For once in my life I didn't have anyone forcing me to do something. I didn't have a motive, beyond that of having fun. I just wanted to experience and possibly learn something new. It was shocking how much fun I had at something I had never done before. – BERENICE

Before he reached his teens, Mike used to hang around and watch every time his brother's rock band came over to their house, in rural Maine, for practice.

> Sometimes I would go up and try to mess around with the drum kit—I really didn't know how to play or anything. I would just bang on stuff and try to play beats like I heard my brother's drummer playing. That was the first I really got a taste of it, and then in eighth grade I decided I wanted to play an instrument. So I eventually got a drum set myself. – MIKE

The company of their peers made almost any activity more compelling, these teenagers said, even when they risked embarrassment by trying.

> It depends on the people in the group, how cool they make you feel. With after-school martial arts I didn't want to do it. And some

of the people there was like, "Come on, try it. It might be fun." And it *was* fun. Messing up is a fun thing too if you can laugh at yourself. It's like you're not being laughed *at*, you're being laughed *with*. — ARIEL B.

I first tried singing with a group of my friends who came over to my house and were all just singing and having fun. I can honestly say I am not good at singing at all, but they forced me and just told me to sing quietly. It was so great knowing I could be bad at something and have fun doing it without being criticized. — AVELINA

Kasia felt sure she would embarrass herself at the ice skating rink, but she risked it because she was in a trusted group of other novices. They would have fun, she decided, even if they fell all over each other.

It is even more fun when the other people who are doing the activity are also first-timers. When you make mistakes you can laugh at each other and it is more comfortable and easygoing for everyone. — KASIA

For Molly, role-playing video games offered a combination of social pleasures and mental challenges.

I play strategy-type games, like "Zelda." It's a quest to save the princess and you're just one character. You have to complete puzzles, figure out how to get to different places. There's not always just one way you can do it—it's a combination of a lot of thinking and a little bit of luck. — MOLLY

She often joins fellow gamers, not just online but in person.

You always have your group of gamer buddies that you play with—even if you're playing a first-person-shooter, you end up playing with your friends. You compare where you've gotten, how fast you've gotten there, what kind of weapons you used—it's very much discussed with your friends. I've played a lot of video games with my friends all together on different machines. Or we play multiplayer games as well, all playing against each other together on the same machine. — MOLLY

Outdoor play can also combine competitive challenges with social fun, Kellie said. She first learned to jump rope with her play-mates on the sidewalks of New York. Right away the complicated maneuvers of Double Dutch had her mesmerized.

When I first saw my friends jump Double Dutch, it made me curi-ous to learn. The first thing I had to know was when to jump in, to get inside of the rope. My sister helped me by counting from one to three or five. I would jump in from the right side, between the rhythm of the ropes or the count in my head, and the rope closest to me had to be in the air. It would usually take me so long that the turners would stop turning and look at me! — KELLIE

Kellie played at Double Dutch every day after school for nearly an hour, hoping to join a team sponsored by the Children's Aid Society.

I would look and see how long my friends were in the rope and that would encourage me to try staying in the rope for more than three minutes. Some of my friends saw that I was struggling and offered to help me, which actually worked. The day of the compe-tition I made it to one hundred steps in the rope and I was so proud of myself. Even though I needed about twenty more steps to make it to the finals, I didn't care. This was the best day of my life! — KELLIE

Sometimes even seemingly passive activities, such as watching television, sparked a desire in some of my student collaborators to learn more about something. In eighth grade, as he watched anime videos while recuperating from injuries he suffered in a car accident, Marquis got interested in Japan.

> I figured, why don't I find out what the anime subtitles are saying? At the end of the video you could go to this web site if you wanted to learn Japanese, but they weren't teaching much. – MARQUIS

Marquis was already planning his own path to mastering the language. He began to imagine an adventurous future unfolding.

> You go downtown and there's this great Japanese store with all these items on sale and stuff. But in there they only speak Japanese. You go in once, you have a small conversation, but the owner says things that you don't know. Now you go home, you study for five days. You come back. You have a longer conversation. Longer, longer, and then all of a sudden he's offered you a job there! – MARQUIS

As these young people describe how they found their compelling interests, they are reminding us that fun—especially when it involves challenge and companionship—is an essential element that propels learning. Though an activity may start as play, kids are also discovering new pleasures they value: solving problems, collaborating with peers, and wielding new skills that could take them into unknown territory.

TRYING IT OUT AT SCHOOL

Whether in the classroom or in extracurricular clubs, many of my student collaborators found opportunities to try something new and interesting at school. Here again their relationships with adults or peers often provided the impetus to get started—and again fun was often a factor.

It Starts with a Spark!

A discussion exercise for adults and youth

Write down something you enjoy doing and want to get better at:

_____

What first got you interested in trying it? Check all the answers that apply, and add your own thoughts on what motivated you. Then share your thoughts with the group.

It looked like fun!

- ☐ It seemed like something you could probably do
- ☐ It involved peers you wanted to be with
- ☐ Success didn't all depend on you
- ☐ No one would be judging you, so the stakes were low

Someone supported and encouraged you at the start

- ☐ They broke it down into steps
- ☐ They did it with you
- ☐ They praised your small successes
- ☐ They showed you how to do better

The activity had an audience that mattered to you

- ☐ At work or school
- ☐ Among friends or family
- ☐ In a public setting

You had a personal interest in getting good at it

- ☐ To express yourself
- ☐ To grow into who you want to be
- ☐ To feel the pleasure of mastering new challenges

◆ NOTE: *To download this worksheet as a pdf, please go to www.firesinthemind.org*

Monte's eleventh-grade English teacher in his Chicago school noticed that Monte was always writing poetry in his free time. Because the class was studying Shakespeare, the teacher tried introducing Monte to dramatic writing too.

> My teacher told me you could combine poetry with playwriting—make up a topic and put yourself in somebody else's shoes and make up a character. Then just go along with that. It was difficult, because I wasn't used to writing no plays—I just write poems. And then he was displaying it like, "Poetry actually can be a play." Because if you're writing one stanza, that could be a piece of a play. It just adds stage direction, like what emotions you want the characters to have saying their lines. So it's like somebody was reading your poetry, just in play terms. – MONTE

As Monte absorbed the comparisons between a Shakespeare play and his own work, his teacher nudged him one step further.

> Playwriting, it helped me, because it made it easy for me to write essays for schoolwork. I could take an idea and combine it with another part, and it come out to one big essay. I put a question in there to get the reader's attention, so they could understand my point of view without using "I" in the essay. They think, "Oh, I know what this writer's talking about." – MONTE

In San Antonio, Bridget began her high school's basic course in economics just as the world economy began its downward plunge.

> I just became all-consumed with economics. With the crises that are going on, all the news and the legislation, it sparked this huge interest in me. It's such a big concern for everyone, looking at those economic choices of the future—especially with college coming up, how you're going to pay for it. – BRIDGET

Bridget got into long conversations about the stock market with her father, who is in business. She quickly realized how much she had to learn.

> You have to be good at analyzing a market, knowing how things will affect basic supply and demand, and what legislation can do to help this or harm it. Right now I have a limited knowledge base, so I'm looking forward to building the skills in it. I want to major in economics in college, and I'm actually looking into maybe doing something with the Federal Reserve when I get out, either being an analyst for them or teaching monetary policy. – BRIDGET

Molly, our video-game enthusiast, also belonged to her school's robotics club, in which students build robots to compete in regional and national contests. She eats, drinks, and sleeps robots for much of the year, Molly said. She had joined the team because "it would look good on my college resume." As time went on, however, the group's united spirit and commitment drew her deeper into the work.

> Everybody is just so dedicated to seeing this robot go from the drawing board to this six-foot-tall, 120-pound robot competing out on the field. It becomes inbred in you to think these engineering things through thoroughly and try to plan things out as much as possible. After you have left the robot, you go home and that's the last thing you think about when you sleep. – MOLLY

By year's end, Molly said, the robotics program had changed her thinking in fundamental ways.

> I never thought about being an engineer; I'm not sure it comes naturally to me. But I look at the world now and I see things that I want to change, and I work towards that as a problem and think through it. – MOLLY

Christian signed up for the Advanced Placement art history course at his Long Beach high school mostly because he too wanted a strong college application. His favorite subject is math and he aspires to be an engineer. "I'm not an artistic person, I'm not that great at art," he said. But in class his teacher drew him in by telling the stories behind many of the paintings.

> For example, "The Raft of Medusa" has a political commentary. It was a ship that sank because the French government placed an unskilled sailor to ship a lot of people. And many people died; it's this grotesque scene with all the people dying, trying to wave at a ship to be saved. — CHRISTIAN

As he came to know more paintings, Christian began to enjoy making his own artistic judgments.

> When I get in depth into the art, I start thinking how the artist would feel when he was doing the painting. Maybe he made the bodies big and solid and strong to show the power of the people, how much hope they had. It's kind of cool. — CHRISTIAN

That same thrill of independent thinking pulled many others toward a particular niche at school. Rachel C.'s suburban high school in Northern California offers an unusual four-year theater curriculum that has students writing, directing, and producing their own plays as well as directing and producing the classics. Rachel was drawn to its intense and unconventional ethos of questioning oneself and the surrounding world.

> You can't survive in theater, in art, if you are complacent or satisfied about what you've been doing. And in that way you make yourself the enemy—because you're always trying to improve upon

yourself and there's no way that you can be content. You may be happy, but that's a different definition. – RACHEL C.

The theater program's emphasis on authentic self-expression, Rachel found, also moved her into a new relationship with her academic studies.

Theater isn't busywork. I feel myself constantly questioning the purpose of why we do the things we do: if it's math, if it's studying science. The only way you can practice theater is through the experience. We're not sitting there at desks, looking at great texts. We're actually getting on stage with those texts and *doing* something with them. – RACHEL C.

And although her interest may have originated with her introspective streak, the drama program also broadened and deepened Rachel's skills and knowledge.

We have to not only perform in a show but also design, manage tech, or run crew on a main-stage production. You need to understand everything that goes behind the performance, and you gain greater respect for it by doing a job that you wouldn't necessarily have done. – RACHEL C.

Each of these students' schools provided a palette of possibilities—curricular or extracurricular—that could encourage and expand something the young person already valued. And because of that chance to learn, an initial spark of interest grew.

A PLACE IN THE COMMUNITY

For many of my student collaborators, an opportunity in the community provided the supportive structure they needed in order to find or develop an area of expertise. Shaw, for example, dropped out of his Oakland high school before he graduated.

> All my friends know that every time you see me, if I'm not listening to music I'm probably banging on something. My friend was, like, "There's a place called Youth Radio where you can get paid to make beats." – SHAW

Shaw stopped into the nonprofit's downtown offices to apply, and soon he was exploring its high-tech music-making systems along with other local students. From there he joined a cohort that was learning broadcasting production skills. Within six months he had a paid internship at the organization, teaching newer students the communication media skills that he was still learning himself.

His new skills in radio mattered less to Shaw than the confidence and leadership he was developing as he advanced. Starting their teaching by focusing on Shaw's original interest, his instructors at Youth Radio conveyed a steady belief that his goals mattered, and that with support and education he could achieve them. At the same time, the organization provided mentorship and auxiliary courses that helped him think through future possibilities.

> I know I'm getting better in music production, but when it comes to my career, I want to be a football coach. I'll be getting my GED and then I plan on attending community college. – SHAW

Rachel M. grew up doing gymnastics, beginning when she was only two years old and reaching an advanced level of competition while still in elementary school. By high school, however, Rachel decided that the all-consuming gymnastics lifestyle had shut off other important things. She wanted to test herself in new ways that mattered more to the community. Her political interest caught fire in the excitement of the 2008 presidential race, and she volunteered with the Democratic campaign headquarters in San Antonio.

> They told me on my first day at the campaign headquarters, "You're going to have people ask you why, and you're going to

have to defend yourself when they tell you that you're wrong." So I
had to do a lot of research about social welfare and taxes and all
the economics, and thankfully I had lots of people helping me out
with that. — RACHEL M.

The election left Rachel determined to continue her work in politics.
She began working on her public speaking skills and researching
possible summer internships in Washington.

Joe too takes pleasure in drawing people into a common cause.
He loves to find different ways of explaining things, and even in his
teens he can tell he makes a good teacher. When he found a job as a
counselor at his Maine community's youth recreation program, he
worked hard but felt in his element.

I have to make it an okay place for anybody to walk in and just be
there, coexist, have fun, be safe. If one kid is not liking it, it means
I haven't done my job right, but at the same time I have to make
sure everything runs smoothly. It's really hard to find that balance
of fun and productivity when you've got five sixth-graders playing
dodgeball with ten kindergartners. We all try and work really hard
to make it a great and positive place, and it hurts me personally—
and I can tell it hurts the other people—when we see the kids
aren't having fun. — JOE

As these young people tried out new interests in community
settings, they were also seeing that both they and their work could
make a difference to others. In ways that might not have happened at
home, school, or play, they began to recognize the reasons to take
their learning further.

A PRIVATE WORLD BECKONS

As a very young child, Evangelina remembers, she would sit and
page through the picture books her mother gave her.

> I don't remember much about how I started to read, how I was interested, how I ended up loving the world I couldn't create on my own. All I remember is liking the pictures, trying to understand what was going on, what the words meant. Word by word, sentence by sentence, little by little, I started to understand. I had a habit of trying not to see, trying not to realize what was going on around me. It was my only escape and it invited me in, it didn't hurt, it wasn't a bad thing. – EVANGELINA

Most of my student collaborators have described some social quality that drew them to the activities they took up and practiced. But some, like Evangelina, found themselves compelled to explore a more interior or creative pleasure, requiring no companion.

> [The story] wasn't real to me, but I wanted to pretend that it was. It was as if someone was talking to me, someone was there to tell me what was going on, taking me into a place where I didn't belong, but a world that I liked. I felt the need to have a certain memory of that experience, even if it wasn't mine. – EVANGELINA

Denise too said that her interest in drawing began as a solitary refuge. She took up paper and pencil at a young age, to "express myself in a way I only knew."

> I only drew when I was angry, because somehow the drawing would always come out better that way. My life was not easy, so I needed something to do to make it unique and yet understandable in my view. No one really helped me at it. I would rip up about four sheets before I finally was done with every little detail, every little line, and I saw on paper what I had in my head. – DENISE Q.

Later in the book we will hear more about how students took these more private pastimes forward, often involving a teacher and an audience. For now we simply note that they too started because the opportunity to explore an inner longing came to hand just at the necessary moment.

JUST BECAUSE IT MATTERS

As we listen to these young people tell of getting started in an area of mastery, we can hear in their voices how much each new role or skill mattered to them. Something they valued—perhaps a family tradition passed down, a place among their peers, a curiosity satisfied, a feeling expressed, or a product they made themselves—always gave meaning and momentum to those first steps into learning.

In that respect, we have as much to learn as they did from their early experiences. We study their stories not because they will predict these students' prowess in other fields; the interests and activities of youth do not dictate their work in the future. Instead, we are looking for a *pattern* of learning that can guide us, whatever we hope to teach them. As we introduce students to algebra or science or history or literature, we can think back to that thing we noticed they valued. Here too it might supply just the right reason for them to step tentatively forward, ready to try.

Many Interests, Many Strengths

Discussion prompts for students and teachers

For youth:

What are you good at that your teachers may not have noticed? When did you start it, and why? Make some notes about it here:

_____

_____

_____

_____

For teachers:

Think about one class of students you teach. Next to the following areas of interest, write the names of those students who you notice have strength in that area:

Sports and physical challenges (basketball, Double Dutch, acrobatics, martial arts)

_____

_____

Arts (music, dance, visual arts, drama)

_____

_____

Crafts (knitting, sewing, carpentry, cooking, and so on)

_____

_____

Logic/puzzles/games (computer or other games, chess, Rubik's Cube, and so on)

_____

_____

Communication (reading, writing, questioning, listening, languages, telling or drawing stories/jokes/comics/cartoons)

_____

_____

Nature, science, gardening, animals

_____

_____

Life skills (wayfinding, caregiving, service, collaboration, friendship, entrepreneurship, management, politics)

_____

_____

If there are students whose strengths you are not sure of, write their names here:

_____

_____

How could you learn more about the strengths, interests, habits, affinities, pastimes, hopes, families, neighborhoods, and cultures of these students?

_____

_____

◆ NOTE: *To download this worksheet as a pdf, please go to www.firesinthemind.org*

CHAPTER THREE

Keeping at It

AS YOUNG PEOPLE introduced their compelling interests to us in Chapter Two, you might have felt a pang of envy at their initial youthful excitement. Which of us would not want to hear that same energy and commitment as they speak of learning at school?

Yet we also well know—and kids do too—how soon a student's initial momentum in any fascinating field can give way to discouraging struggles. We heard students briefly refer to those hard parts as they described their beginnings in an area of engagement. In this chapter, they tell what helped them stick with their learning journeys, despite the stumbling blocks.

We will hear these teenagers give their reasons—not so different from our own—for wanting to get better at what first captured their interest. They describe their satisfaction in striving to meet a goal they cared about, and their pleasure and pride in even their small successes. And as we move through various aspects of their pursuit of different goals and satisfactions, we will

> **WHAT KIDS TELL US**
>
> You need a hater and you need a motivator. The person that's telling you that you can't do it—that's your hater, and you want to prove them wrong. And your motivator is the person that's supporting you. You try your best so you can make your motivator proud.
>
> — LONYA

see the powerful effect that the right kind of practice has on young people—increasing their belief that they can succeed and their motivation to keep at it.

IT'S WORTH THE TROUBLE

Ever since Jewel was a child, she really wanted to be a doctor. Then, in tenth grade, a demanding chemistry course made her doubt that she could stay on such a difficult academic track. She dreaded going into eleventh-grade biology, at first.

> But then some lab experiments we did really made me think, "This is what I want to do." In one, we got bacteria off the door handle in the girls' bathroom, and we had to bring something from home that we thought could kill it. We put it in a petri dish and watched it over time. And when I saw that my experiment worked, it made me think, "Imagine doing this on a bigger scale, like with a human body, and actually curing something." So now, even though biology might be hard at first, I just keep practicing. Realizing how much it applies to the real world—to people—makes it more interesting and just keeps me going through it. – JEWEL

Jewel knows she has many years of arduous study ahead if she is to fulfill her dream. But like many other students she is sticking with it, because the hard parts connect to a result she can clearly visualize.

That reward need not be a career, however, and it need not take years to achieve. Conjugating French verbs, for example, had little appeal for Kenzie, the soccer player. But when his French class organized a trip to France, he worked hard to move his language skills to the next level.

> I needed some end result to reach towards—a little push from behind makes it a lot easier to do the stuff you're made to do right

now. If you don't imagine anything coming out of what you're learning, then you're not going to give it your best. – KENZIE

Even modest results that they could look at immediately—like Avelina's square of knitting that was growing into a scarf—gave students a sense that their efforts were worth continuing.

When you're first starting off, it's really frustrating. You're just sitting down and concentrating on it. But watching it progress, you actually get to see your work becoming something. First it's a little block, but it gets longer and becomes a rectangle, and then it becomes really long, and soon you can wrap it around your neck! – AVELINA

For other students, the value of sticking with it lay in moments when the intrinsic qualities of their actions yielded deep satisfaction and fulfillment. Rodrigo, who plays in his school orchestra, said that the music itself rewarded his efforts to master difficult passages.

Our expectation is to be a musician, not just get some noise out of an instrument. So when somebody's struggling, we ask for help and support from each other. Our motivation is the passion for music itself—being part of an orchestra making music. – RODRIGO

Dylan said that his long daily run along the country roads of Maine gave him a steady grounding for everything else he did in his day. It was "a practice" in a different sense, he suggested.

Running is something that I always want to do. Whether I'm supposed to or not, I just get out there and get on the roads and run every day. – DYLAN

Intellectual satisfaction also counted as a result worth striving for. Kathryn, working on a demanding school project in global studies, took pride in the demonstrable body of knowledge that she could call her own.

I gathered a lot of background information and connected it to my question. And I also have new knowledge that I gained while researching the question and taking it further. Now I feel like I can talk about it almost like an expert! – KATHRYN

These students' stories show us that the pleasures of accomplishment can sustain them long before they reach their ultimate goal. As they savor each moment of success, we can help them connect it to those moments that came before—and those that will follow.

WATCHING THE BEST

Whatever their field of interest, many of my young collaborators said they watched closely what old hands were doing in their fields, taking in their standards of excellence and analyzing their every action.

Berenice attended a summer program at Villanova University, where she took courses in extemporaneous speaking and essay writing. The work was hard, so she decided to scrutinize the work of others for examples of how to do it well.

I had trouble starting and ending different kinds of writing, like speeches, essays, research papers, or memoir. What helped was that I like to read other people's work, and I could observe how their structure was different from mine. I know I'm not the best writer, but I have improved a lot. By the time I left I had about twelve speeches written, and I knew how to write under pressure. – BERENICE

In the San Antonio restaurant kitchen where Karen worked, each plate had to meet first the head chef's standards and then those of the customer. She learned to look carefully at what succeeded and to imitate it.

My boss is a perfectionist: it has to be perfect, no matter what. You can't restart, because it takes so long for certain meats to be prepared. When we get it done, some of us stand at the door and watch the customer eat it. We pray that they like it! If they don't, our pay gets deducted. If they do, we get a raise. – KAREN

Shaquasia's sister and cousins would make up dances to the latest songs on the radio. They didn't have time to teach her the steps as they created them, but she didn't want to feel like an outsider in a house where everybody danced. She studied their moves intently, then went looking for more.

I would watch videos really closely and try to do all the steps the dancers were doing and count the beats of the song. And I would ask my mother to teach me the dances she did in her teenage years, because many dances came from her generation. – SHAQUASIA

When Andrew first took up skateboarding, for instance, he had nobody to help him. Reluctant to look like a rank beginner in a New York City public park, he sought out every opportunity to learn from the moves of experienced skaters.

At first I pretty much guessed and kept trying when nobody else was around. Then I saw some skate videos and video games, to see how they jump. They keep pushing their back foot hard, then lean forward with the front foot, so I kept trying to do that. Sometimes I would leave my board at home and go out to watch others. And in a week, I finally was able to jump. – ANDREW

No matter where it took place, their close observation and analysis of good work by others helped students demystify the expertise they aspired to. Their exemplars gave them authentic criteria for excellence—and a realistic picture of the deliberate, step-by-step practice that underlies everyone's journey to mastery.

TO PROVE YOU CAN

These teenagers found great satisfaction in pulling off something hard, especially against the odds. Lusaida's father, an auxiliary police officer, got her interested in law enforcement and in ninth grade she signed up for a youth program at his precinct. When she first saw what it entailed, she wondered if she could go through with it.

> I had many laws to memorize and marches to learn and at first it was too much for me. I was ready to quit, until my officer adviser motivated me to keep on. He told me that new things get hard, but with the right thinking it will no longer be a hassle but something I enjoy. That made me want to keep going, and since I was getting good at it, I devoted myself even more. Now I'm out there putting safety in people's lives! – LUSAIDA

Many of my students said they worked hard at something just to prove themselves to others. Lonya, who hopes to be "a famous dancer," said that both scoffers and supporters made her determined to keep practicing, even when she felt insecure.

> You need a hater and you need a motivator. The person that's putting you down, telling you that you can't do it—that's your hater, and you want to prove them wrong. And your motivator is the person that's supporting you. You try your best on everything so you can make your motivator proud. – LONYA

Gymnastics practice took up most of Rachel's free time in her early teens, holding her back in other parts of her life. But when her parents urged her to discontinue the sport, she only grew more committed.

> I had to eat a certain way, I couldn't go to parties, I had to do things a certain way at school—that was the hardest part for me.

And my parents always said, "You know, you can quit." One of the big things that motivated me was that they didn't see a point in it. I told them frequently, "Why would you want me to quit? This is something I love, this is something I am good at." And so I worked hard and I proved them wrong. – RACHEL M.

Even playful teasing from peers spurred some students to push on. Odell, the poet, sometimes felt that others disrespected his versifying, but their scoffing made him work even harder at it.

Sometimes it gets to me when people make fun of me because I do something different. But in a way it just inspires me to do better. – ODELL

When Andris took up cooking, her family laughed at the results. She felt gleeful vindication as she finally learned to put successful meals on the table.

When I first began, my brothers and uncles made fun of me, like, "You can't do it, you're going to poison somebody!" Now the people that teased me is the same people that want me to cook for them! – ANDRIS

That same desire to prove themselves to others—whether they were hopeful or dubious—also came up in school according to several students from rural Maine. Brandie, for example, said she hates to disappoint her teachers.

If they care about you, they're going to be, "Aw, you could have done better; I'm kind of disappointed in you." It makes me feel like crap and it makes me want to do better later to impress them again. – BRANDIE

Tough-talking athletic coaches galvanized her classmate Joe to work harder.

Two of my coaches really scare the living daylights out of me. They'll flat-out say that you're not living up to your best potential: "I tried to make you a good athlete, but you just want to screw around." It makes you feel bad—you don't want to seem like a waste of their time. So I try and do the best I can. I don't want to make them angry. – JOE

And Dylan's teacher struck a similarly stern note, but with a warm undercurrent.

The first class of the year he actually came out and said, "If you want to be here, you'll show me that in your work and your effort and your class participation." Before assignments he says, "You better step up and show that you want to be here and that you want to be learning." It kind of showed me that, all right, if I want him to help me through this, I'm going to have to show him that I'm willing to learn. – DYLAN

In all of these stories we can see the strong push that other people's expectations and opinions—sometimes positive, sometimes negative—exert on the students involved. Against those dynamic social currents, adolescents are continually defining themselves, deciding what they want to practice and what they will set aside.

MASTERY LOVES COMPANY

That social factor also showed up in high relief when teenagers talked about working on difficult tasks in a group of their peers. Tackling those challenges alongside others made their hardships almost fun, they said.

Physics isn't really for everyone, and the teacher knew that. But everyone loves ice-skating, and so for one of our field trips in physics we went ice-skating. For a while we skated for fun, and then we had to do physics experiments on the ice—calculating speed and all sorts of different physics. Doing that with my friends in that type of learning environment made it a lot more enjoyable. I still remember a lot of the methods for calculating velocity and acceleration. – RACHEL M.

As Dan, an eighth grader in New York City, practiced his moves with the school's ballroom dance team, he drew confidence from his fellow dancers.

For me, it's actually easier when a lot of people in the class *don't* know what's going on. You say, "Oh, they're making a mistake, so maybe I could work on that for me a little more." And then once you do it, it bounces back to them and they see it, so it's much more of a working community. It's like in order to jump you need to bend your knees; you can't jump just standing still. In order to get somewhere, you have to notice what you're doing wrong. – DAN

The teenage members of a Providence community music program's string quartet said that friendships kept them involved, even as the music-making grew more difficult. For eight years Kirby showed up for lessons, largely because "it's where I feel most comfortable," she said.

But I wasn't driven to practice on a regular basis until I joined the quartet with these guys a few months ago, and then I realized I had to step it up. I started to practice every single day. And now I just do it. – KIRBY

Sometimes only teamwork allowed my young collaborators to stick with something hard, building skills and knowledge one step at a time. Matthew, a Long Beach student, had an acquaintance who set up a web-based sales site and asked him to help maintain it. Neither of them had all the skills they needed to do the job right, so the two relied on each other continually.

> At first it was very hard to put the new products in. I kept having to go over and over it. But we were both doing it at the same time, so he was usually there to consult about things I learned and things he learned. We put our information together and we would build on that. — MATTHEW

Patty and her sister both play softball and Patty said that each compensates for the other's weaker area.

> I'm not so good at catching but my sister is. She is not good at pitching but I am. We become an important part of the team because pitching and catching is about 75 percent of the softball game. — PATTY

Aaron typically falls asleep over his homework within ten minutes, he said—unless he has a study partner.

> I can't study by just cracking open a book; I'll be like, "Man, this is boring!" For me to sit down with somebody and actually go over it makes it a whole lot easier. If it's something he don't know, then I can tell him, and if it's something I don't know, then he can tell me. We quiz each other on what we're reading, so it's a win-win situation. It's interesting and you're learning at the same time. — AARON S.

Looking at these scenarios, it's easy to see how young people's motivation increases when they are working on new skills and knowledge in a companionable setting. They are gaining early practice in the habits of the "expert team," a concept we will continue to explore in later chapters.

Some Reasons for Keeping at It

"I'll make them proud."	The desire to prove your motivator right
"I'll prove them wrong."	The desire to prove your "hater" wrong
"I did it!"	A climactic moment of achievement
"It's what I do."	A series of plateaus with steady and satisfying work (often with others)
"I could come in first!"	The adrenalin surge that comes with competition
"I'll get respect."	Public recognition of your accomplishment
"I *know* this!"	The satisfying moments when you can feel that you know

COMPETING WITH RIVALS

Even though they enjoyed collaborating, these teenagers told me, they often compared themselves to others—even if only privately. Bridget considers the competitive spirit to be hardwired.

> I think people don't necessarily want to be good at something just for the knowledge and proficiency. I think we have a drive to be recognized and set apart—number one, the best. – BRIDGET

Tysheena was used to performing before audiences with the ballroom dance group, but a citywide competition bumped her effort level up a notch.

> Competing, there's always something kind of bigger than when you're performing. I think the competition maybe gets me more

motivated. I know that in the end I might win or lose, so it makes me try harder. — TYSHEENA

For Aaron, the drive to win at basketball justified all his exhausting efforts in practice.

I could be really, really tired jogging up the basketball court, but if I'm down by two points and the game's almost over, I need to get somehow, some way to win that game. Everything else is tuned out. That's the only thing I'm focused on, whether it's assisting somebody or making the shot myself or just playing defense, I'm going to do it. — AARON S.

Molly plays video games just for fun, she said. Still, she presses herself continually to improve her strategies and drive up her scores.

It's really a matter of skill. Your first score may be a matter of luck, but then you're continually getting better and better, a steady incline of your score. If you beat an entire game, you can go back to see if you can make your score better. That's a lot of the drive to play; it's a lot of fun to compare your scores to other people's, to try and make yourself better. — MOLLY

Darrian, an expert chess player at fourteen, agrees that creating a winning strategy constitutes the pleasure of the game itself, for her.

Chess is like a duel. You have to think about every single thing. But it's not just enjoying the win—I really like figuring out *how* to win. — DARRIAN

Not every activity lends itself to competition, and some of my students cared more about winning than others. But for those who wanted to be "number one, the best," rivalry fueled a drive to keep on practicing.

RECOGNITION BY A COMMUNITY

Recognition and appreciation within their various communities also helped these students stick with an arduous effort. Tysheena said that her place on a team gave her a special status in eighth grade.

> I have a title now: "Oh, she's on the ballroom dance team."
> — TYSHEENA

The notice and praise that spurred young people on often started with family and friends. Denise began drawing as a child and kept it up because she saw that others liked her work.

> The hardest part when I first began was knowing if I was really good or just a wannabe. My mother finally told me my drawings were beautiful, and my friends kept telling me that I was actually good at it. Once I realized what other people thought, I decided that I would challenge myself even more. — DENISE Q.

Henry started cooking at his mother's knee. By thirteen he had plenty of practice in serving his own dishes to family and guests.

> It makes you feel really good when their face lights up and they say, "Oh, this is really good, I love it." And when they start asking questions: "Oh, how'd you do this?" You feel like you've mastered another skill. — HENRY

Avelina, the tenth-grade knitter, liked standing out in a group when she wore something she had created herself.

> It makes you feel very different, special, because not everybody knits. So when you're wearing the scarf and people ask you, "Where did you get it?" you can say, "I made it with my own hands." It's something that's *you*, it's unique. It gives you a sense of accomplishment. You can be proud of it. — AVELINA

Public notice provided a push to practice for Kirby and Joshua, in the Providence music program. Joshua said that his viola playing opened many doors for him.

> It's definitely pushing me to take more leadership roles. They ask all the students if they want to join the philharmonic and the youth orchestra here in Rhode Island. This is my fourth year in that, and I want to go into symphony next year. — JOSHUA R.

And Kirby said she took her cello practice much more seriously when the string quartet had a big concert coming.

> It's not that they didn't expect a lot—I just didn't expect a lot from myself. But now I was playing on this big stage alongside my teachers. I'm in a quartet, and we're the lead players in orchestra. — KIRBY

Other students also said that an audience served as a big motivator. Tessa had a passion for writing, but she also found it stressful to get her ideas into the form she wanted. When she first found an online publisher for her poetry, she took heart.

> I put a couple of my favorites on Poetry.com, where a lot of people read them. And I got a letter back saying they wanted to put it in the books that they were putting together. I was like, "Wow, somebody's actually noticing what I'm doing." And it made me want to write more poetry so I could be recognized more. — TESSA

Public honor for hard work, these stories show us, provides a powerful form of encouragement—and it need not come as the climax of their labors. At every point along their paths, the praise of others for hard-earned progress made these adolescent learners feel not just pride but the desire to go even further.

ENCOURAGEMENT EQUALS EXPECTATION

So far in these chapters, my student collaborators have told us a lot about what they want to get good at, and why. We can hear in their stories how much it means to them to someday take their places as accomplished persons in fields they care about. And we can see how clearly they imagine the pleasure, satisfaction, and triumph of achieving that.

Yet despite how much value they placed on succeeding at something, these kids often lost confidence that they could do it. At many frustrating points along the way they felt like giving up. In this section they show us how some encouraging person guided them past that point by giving them an engaging task that lay just beyond—but not too far beyond—their skill level.

As we hear those stories, long-established research from cognitive science springs to life. We can see their crisis of confidence pass as a teacher sets the bar at just the right height. And we can see these young people realize that they can expect to master each successive step, with practice.

> In the beginning stage of learning something new, you really need full-on support, 'cause it gives you the strength to keep doing it even if you do mess up. – ALEXIS

Erika, who took dance lessons for years, described different ways such moments can play out.

> Some teachers just throw steps and choreography at you. They don't seem to really care about whether or not you get it. You could be in the back of the class struggling and they only focus on the ones in the front of the room who get it. Like, "Okay, those are the ones who are gonna make it." But then I've had teachers who take the ones struggling in the back and make them come up to the

front, and they show them what they need to do. They like to point out what you're doing right too. That can be inspiring, that can be what takes a student from "Oh, I can't do this" to "Wow, I might want to make a career out of this." – ERIKA

Many students needed such technical instruction in a certain skill to get them past these discouraging moments. But just as much, they said, they wanted reassurance that they should expect such setbacks as a perfectly normal part of getting better.

Mike, for instance, acquired a feel for the drums by watching his brother's band practice. In the beginning he taught himself to play, but before long he knew he needed a teacher.

> I just didn't have the coordination to do a double-stroke roll, where your stick bounces once on the snare, like "buh-*bum*," and you hit the other stick and it bounces. Ideally it gets going really fast, so you can get two strokes with one hit. My teacher told me that you just have to go slow and play that forever until you understand the movement. Then once you get comfortable with it, you just work your way up, play a little bit faster, and then just a little bit faster. I started every day to practice and practice and practice, and then I could do it. – MIKE

Ninoshka learned to knit from her grandmother, "hand on hand." The older woman's warm belief in her came through with every stitch, she said.

> She really wasn't trying to help me much. She told me that I would catch on really fast because I am good with hands-on things, like beads. I liked that my grandmother had confidence in me; she really believed that I was going to get far into it. She said that I should make her something, and I really wanted to do something special for her. She would not be mad at me, no matter what came out wrong, because she was trying to make me better at it. – NINOSHKA

Brandie became disheartened by the sheer quantity of writing that her teacher asked the class to do in seventh and eighth grade. She kept it up, in part because the teacher's responses always included appreciative words about Brandie's personal strengths.

> She had a bulletin board and at the end of the week she'd write you a really nice note about your work, and about you in general. She'd fold the notes up with your name on them, so nobody else could read them. I kept a couple of them, and I know somebody who kept *all* of them. – BRANDIE

Janiy's piano teacher also warmly encouraged her through difficult periods. Slowly Janiy was cultivating the habit of persistence, she realized.

> Some days I don't want to wake up and have my piano teacher there. But there's times when I try to give up and she's there telling me, "You can do this." And when you practice and you finally get it, it's a great sense of accomplishment. You can make the person who's sitting next to you proud, and show the world that you're not a quitter. Piano is just a hobby, but it's good practice—it can help you become stronger, because there's larger obstacles in life that you have to face, where you must stick with it to move on. – JANIY

At moments when students faltered, such encouragement went beyond emotional support. Almost always it came from people who knew what they were talking about because they had climbed the same ladder themselves. They knew what next step each student was ready for, and when to give a skill time to develop. Their lack of anxiety about whether the student could do it also raised the young person's own expectation of success—and bolstered the will to practice that would fulfill that expectation, in good time.

BUILDING ON BELIEF

Like Janiy, many other students told me that their efforts were making them stronger at what they had set out to do. As they mastered each new skill or concept, they began to believe that they could accomplish even more. And their stories reveal a powerful connection between their deliberate practice and their increasing motivation.

Mike took his girlfriend, Samantha, out to a nearby mountain to teach her how to snowboard. Sam was a rank beginner and she described how Mike approached her earliest mistakes.

> I had just fallen down, when I was trying to turn. And he came and helped me up and told me that I had ridden a little bit farther than I had before. He told me that I was doing good and I just needed to work a little bit more on [turning]. If he had told me that I needed to change everything, I would have just quit. – SAMANTHA

By noticing Sam's progress, then singling out the specific factor that was blocking her, Mike let her know that she could build on what she did know how to do.

> Then he corrected me on how to turn. It definitely made me feel better, and it pushed me to want to do it again. It was a lot better than just falling down and him picking me up. It's like giving you encouragement *and* correcting you at the same time. – SAMANTHA

Mike's coaching provided Sam with just what she needed to dispel her anxiety. For the first time she began to expect that she could become good at snowboarding if she kept at it.

If Chanel does not get that kind of targeted help near the start of a difficult math problem, she said, she loses confidence in her own ability and her motivation plummets.

> When I get something wrong in math it's like, "I don't want to try it again, because I got it wrong." It makes you feel like you're miss-

ing something, like you can't accomplish it. There's no ending to it because you don't even know how to start it. – CHANEL

By stepping in at the right moment, a teacher or coach can help change young people's mindset about whether they can learn to do something well. "I used to be *painfully* shy," Chelsea, a twelfth grader in Maine, told me with a big laugh. Her first step toward overcoming that handicap came when an eighth-grade teacher prodded her to enter a speech competition with a scholarship as a prize.

I guess I'd always assumed the worst would happen if I spoke up in public. I thought that people were going to walk away or something, even though that's never going to be the case. – CHELSEA

With the coaching she needed, Chelsea raised her voice before an audience for the first time that year. When she got to high school she found the courage to join the speech and debate club.

And slowly I got over it. Nobody was really there to, you know, attack my bad orating skills. They would give me feedback, and I'd work on what they told me to—practicing it an insane amount of times, watching myself in the mirror and pointing out my own flaws. After a while I realized that trying to act confident was actually pretty fun. – CHELSEA

Students who had experiences like this said they gradually started to think of themselves as smarter. Kenzie, the soccer player, told of training his mind before a game, deliberately creating his own expectation that he could carry existing skills and knowledge into new and stressful territory.

A big part of your confidence in the game is imagining yourself actually doing on the field the skills and the plays that you know how to do. Once you get comfortable with the game and you have most of the skills down, it becomes a mental challenge. Sometimes it's hard to translate that from practice to the game. But if you can do it, it becomes a lot easier to play well. – KENZIE

That same mental exercise carried over into other parts of life, observed Aaron, the basketball player from Long Beach. "Whatever you *think* is what your reaction is going to be," he said.

In a certain neighborhood, most likely you're going to die doing something stupid. You're like, "I'm not going to make it, so why not go now?" Or when I'm taking the tests for college I might be like, "The others couldn't do it, so why should I even be here?" But if you tell me that most people actually pass, I'm going to be more confident, like, "Okay, if they can do it, I can do it." It puts you in a completely different mind-set. You force yourself to get what you want because you know you can achieve it. You go from "Oh, I can't do this" to the confidence to do anything. – AARON S.

CHALLENGE CREATES MORE CHALLENGE

Once they began to believe they could excel at something, these students said, they did not always make progress in leaps and bounds. But they actually began to look forward to the long plateaus of practice, where they met the same challenge again and again, ever more familiar with how to approach it. And eventually they grew ready to take new risks by trying something even harder.

Bridget, the San Antonio student with a passion for economics, recalled her frustration with reading in childhood because a learning disability prevented her from associating letters with their sounds. As people helped her to keep at the problem over the years, written language began to make more sense.

It wasn't until I started reading more—started having a hunger for reading and writing—that things started clicking in my brain. Then

I got to be a better student and started really enjoying learning.
— BRIDGET

Coming back to the same difficult activity on a regular basis became a habit with its own satisfactions. Joshua first picked up the viola at age seven, at the community music program in his low-income Providence neighborhood. He bonded with his young teachers and soon simply showing up for practice gave him a sense of becoming an adult as well as a musician. "The strings program taught me how to be committed to something, to not be afraid of challenges," he said. At sixteen his viola studies had become the force driving him toward high school graduation and beyond.

For Dan, practicing on the school's ballroom dance team held a pleasure beyond any contest prize.

When you're matching with the music perfectly, you feel the reward inside you—it's not just, "Oh, I'm winning the competition, we get a trophy." It's almost like an inner trophy that you have. It's an inner win for you. You've overcome something of yourself and you feel proud of yourself for doing it. — DAN

At the same time, these young people were creating in themselves the habit of raising the bar. Marquis described his study of Japanese in those terms.

You look at yourself like in two sides of a mirror: "This is me before, that's me after." And you keep putting this bar above you: "Okay, all I have to do is get from here to here, that's pretty simple." Then you keep moving it up, and now you feel really good: "Hey, I've done this, I'm glad I stuck through that practice." — MARQUIS

Christian, whose art teacher taught him to associate stories with great paintings, began to extend his new analytic habit into other academic areas.

What Makes Us Willing to Try?

A dialogue for teachers with students

What would you like to try but you worry that you wouldn't be good at it?

_____

_____

What conditions would make it feel safe to try that activity?

_____

_____

_____

It can be fun to do something even when it's hard and you're not that great at it. Give an example from your own experience.

_____

_____

_____

Describe a time when you mastered *one step* of a difficult activity because you were *just then* ready for it.

_____

_____

_____

◆ NOTE: *To download this worksheet as a pdf, please go to www.firesinthemind.org*

If it's broken down to something you can understand, then you get attracted to it. Like, this certain painting, *The Death of Marat*, incorporates a political murder scene that the painter saw himself. When you start learning the little details, you're like, "Oh, this painting's really good!" And it's the same thing with math. If you don't understand how to do a problem, you're like, "I don't want to learn it." But when you break it down, you see how easy and interesting it is. — CHRISTIAN

Many of my student collaborators said that each new step in their valued activities gave them a jumping-off point for the next step. Making his own skateboard grew into an intense effort over many weeks, said Tyler, the San Diego student whose grandfather first hooked him on how things worked. On the final day of his project, all distractions dropped away.

I painted it, sanded it, and then I was going to quit because it got dark. Then I realized that I could use a hairdryer to make each coat dry. So I hung a light in the alley, and when the final coat of paint was drying I looked at my watch and it was after eleven. I was like, "Hmm, didn't seem like it was that long." — TYLER

With the skateboard complete, he stepped back to assess it—and immediately had the itch for another challenge.

As soon as I finished it I was like, "How am I going to make the next one better?" — TYLER

Like so many other stories here, Tyler's experience shows the fire that burns in young people when they tackle a problem that matters to them while also expecting that they can surmount its difficulties. But these stories also give us ample evidence that such motivation never arrives on the scene before the stage is set.

If kids do not think a task is important, they will not want to do it, even if they could do it perfectly. And if they do not expect that they can succeed at a task, they also lose the desire to try. Motivation to learn is a *product* of those states of mind, not a precursor. We will see it—in ourselves and in our students—only when two necessary factors combine: *what we value* and *what we expect we can do*.

Listening to young people in these last two chapters, we have identified key conditions that start and sustain their serious practice, whatever they are learning. In many of their scenarios, you may recognize yourself—and the vital importance of your example, your actions, and your encouraging tone when things grow harder. Next, students take our investigation to yet another level as they probe the work of experts to discover exactly what goes into the process of getting really good at what you do.

CHAPTER FOUR

Asking the Experts

N THE LAST CHAPTER, students told us what it took for them to keep at something they were learning, even when things got harder. In their voices we could hear the pride they felt at pushing past difficulties and discovering their own resources and strengths.

Step by step, through the practice of things they valued, each of

these teenagers seemed to be building an identity as an accomplished person. Achieving excellence at something was becoming an important part of who they were.

At the same time they were growing more interested in the expertise of other people in the world around them.

"What's the difference between a surgeon and a jazz musician?" asked Aaron, a student from San Antonio.

> Do they go through the same sort of obstacles, the same process to get to where they are? Do they have the same ideas of what those two things involve? And do they get the same satisfaction, do they get the same sort of feelings and ideas from doing their jobs? – AARON R.

Others wondered if their own process of getting good at something might mirror that of the masters in various fields. Whatever the answer, Ruben said, we should find out more.

> If we know how experts do it, then it's a model for us on how to do whatever we have to do to become an expert in whatever field we choose. The fields might be different, but how you carry yourself to that goal, I think, is going to be similar with everybody. — RUBEN

For this chapter, I asked my teenage collaborators to go looking for that firsthand information from very accomplished adults. What got them started? What kept them going when things got hard? Where did they gather knowledge? Who did they ask for guidance? What did they practice, and how?

These young people had answered these same questions about themselves earlier in our work. They were already developing new perspectives on their own growing knowledge and skills. In taking this next step, they would approach the adult community with new standing: as thinkers, learners, and actors in the pursuit of mastery.

WHO'S AN EXPERT?

Before going out into the field, the students had many discussions about which people they should choose to interview. Few of them knew anyone who had achieved fame, but all knew people who went well beyond "good enough." Who counted as an expert? They brainstormed some possibilities.

> There are two types of people: one who can do everything pretty well and then the person who wants to just be really, really focused on one thing and only put their time into that. — RACHEL W.

Experts have been on that path of refining the skills needed in
their field; they have them down and they can share them with
others. – BRIDGET

Certainly, students said, they would look for people who had
focused for many years in a particular area. And a person's reputation
also mattered. People tend to bring tough problems to those who have
a record of figuring them out.

Their work or ideas are recognized, and they actually have experience with it. It's very different that you know something intellectu-
ally than when you know the facts in reality and can do something
with them. – RODRIGO

However, real experts would not just manage the routine problems
that came their way, said Aaron.

An expert is someone people come to, to ask about their subject matter. But if you are an expert, I think you go the extra level. You need the
curiosity to go further to answer those same questions. – AARON R.

Experts would have an appetite for challenge, the students supposed.
They would always be seeking out more complex problems, new
strategies, creative solutions.

Their job comes like a second nature. They don't have to really say,
"What am I supposed to do next?" They just do it. They may not
learn it by a book or by somebody telling them, but they are doing
it—no matter what, they are going to learn how. – RUBEN

They can make mistakes but they also are quick to learn from their
mistakes. They grow from it and they continue to grow. – ERIKA

Experts should also demonstrate both consistency and adaptability,
we decided. Crystal described how her badminton coach could

"continually hit a direct spot," making him an expert in her eyes. And Kristian, who studied dance, said that her opinion of a choreographer rose or fell depending on whether he could "adapt to the times changing."

> If you are really an expert, you are well enough versed in what you do that you can change. — KRISTIAN

By now these young people could think of many people they might interview: parents, coaches, professionals, tradespeople, farmers, artists, teachers. All of these people stood out at what they did and all seemed to possess the "expert qualities" we had agreed on. Clearly, however, they came from very different backgrounds. Audio recorders in hand, my teenage collaborators went out to find out more about their interview subjects' paths to expertise.

WHERE DO EXPERTS GET THEIR KNOWLEDGE?

All the experts that my students interviewed started by acquiring a crucial fund of information in their fields. We discovered, however, that they did not always learn this fundamental knowledge in school. For example, Ruben told us that his father, the mechanic, was always reading auto repair books and manuals.

> When something changes with how a car works, it's usually one or two things. So he hears about it from the manufacturer, or a magazine will talk about it, or there might be a class he can attend. When he buys parts, they sell books that give specific details on certain things. Sometimes somebody with more knowledge about it would actually show him what to do, but there wasn't always somebody there to help him. — RUBEN

The jazz cornetist interviewed by Rachel had a distinguished career, but he had picked up his formal knowledge in bits and pieces. As a child he listened to old 78-RPM records of classical music, and then a friendly middle-school teacher helped him learn to read notes so he could join the band. His rigorous training did not come until twenty, however, when he would drive for hours to study in a small group with a master player. Those classes were intensely demanding, he told Rachel.

> He would sit on a swivel chair in the middle of our circle, and he would play a simple little exercise, and then he would turn to one of us and make him play what he had just played. And then we would critique them. That lesson would go on for four hours. Nobody got up, nobody got their mind off it. This was seven days a week. – JAZZ CORNETIST

Some experts acquired high-status credentials, then practiced their expertise in an occupation that did not demand them. Kristian interviewed a tattoo artist who had learned his techniques in art school. He told her:

> A lot of the techniques that tattoo artists use are actually things that my professors were teaching me in college. Color theory, different lighting for shadows, highlights, I learned in painting. Even sculpting plays a big part in tattooing, when you are doing realism, a 3D look, because you're trying to sculpt the piece rather than just color in or fill in an area that's outlined. – TATTOO ARTIST

Most of these experts kept seeking out new information as their fields developed. The apple farmer whom Kenzie interviewed in Maine, for example, learned his craft from his father and brother as he grew up. But he was continually taking agricultural extension courses, reading widely, and acquiring new techniques from field researchers and other orchardists.

> My dad has thirty to forty years of experience, but there are some things that you may not have done in the past. You go to seminars

and trade shows to learn additional skills, or new technology comes out that you need to know. And there's an apple specialist and a disease specialist at the University of Maine who are research scientists, so you end up learning that you *don't* know what you *think* you know. – ORCHARDIST

At the same time, students noticed, these experts were continually weaving informal know-how into their base of knowledge. They reached some conclusions by using common sense. They picked up other skills and information by watching people, trying things, and asking questions.

A bowling champion in a West Side Chicago league developed his technique through a patchwork of sources, he told Brianna, the ninth grader who interviewed him.

I started out with an older crowd, so they showed me the basics of the game, and I began watching other people around me bowl. But the more technical things I learned through DVDs, books, and trial and error. Trial and error is the best teacher; I started to see my score increase and my handicap decrease. – BOWLER

Chelsea's father, a hobbyist brewer, took the same approach when he was learning to make beer.

Talking to the owner of the store where I bought my supplies, I learned a lot. There's also a couple of web sites that talk about different methods and different ingredients, different ways of brewing, and you learn things from that. You listen, and you try to come up with your own little concoction and brew something that you like to drink. – BREWER

In some of their interviews, students could see how people built up expertise simply by tuning in to what was around them. A Chicago police detective told Kelvin, a ninth grader, that he continually picked up signals, impressions, and patterns from street-corner behaviors.

> Once my eye developed for the street, I started to get better along the way. You get better at seeing things, you get better at watching people and interpreting their movements and their actions. There's times on the street when I've seen somebody do something that other guys won't take notice of. – DETECTIVE

Knowledge gained in such ways could be hard to explain or teach, we noticed in these interviews. Experts such as this police officer may "just know" what they know, without being able to say exactly why. Yet such people sometimes seemed to organize and build on their informal knowledge by talking about their experiences with others in their field. For example, an experienced teacher told Andris that she relied on this process.

> When I started off teaching I was much more focused on me and my classroom and getting good at what I'm doing. Now I'm more interested in observing other teachers and what kinds of lessons they're doing. There's a lot of sharing that started to go on between myself and the other English teachers. Also, I have friends who are teachers, so they tell me about their classrooms and problems that they have with students. We just kind of talk it out, learning from our mistakes. – HIGH SCHOOL TEACHER

THE HABITS THAT EXPERTS USE

It wasn't enough, these teenagers were realizing, to "know about" something if you wanted to be really good at it. It wasn't even enough to "know how" to do that thing. To really understand what expertise meant, they would have to watch closely what people *did* with the knowledge and skills they had—and how they did it.

Rodrigo realized this when he interviewed his mother, a psychologist.

> She said that the hardest part is actually applying the information you learned in training when you are with a person right in front of you. And it seems that it's very different from being teached the tools than using them on a situation. There's certain things that the person has to learn on their own. – RODRIGO

Perhaps, we thought, we could distill those "certain things" into a list of habits that helped such accomplished people achieve their success. We looked again at the students' interview transcripts and came up with the following possibilities.

Experts ask good questions. To be an expert, Zac surmised, "you have to be curious in the first place—to want to know." No matter how much the people who were interviewed seemed to know, they continued to come up with more questions. They were always turning over the problem in their minds, speculating about the possibilities, asking, "What would happen if. . . ?"

Aaron's mother, an occupational therapist who had practiced for thirty years, told him that this habit of curiosity served her well.

> I deal with so much information and I try to make a picture with it all. I'm constantly taking snapshots, thinking, "Okay, where is this kid? What's the matter? Is it the environment?" You filter a lot of things, notice a lot of things, go through a checklist in your mind. No two patients are alike—that child is completely unique! Piecing together all this information quickly makes you all the better.
> – OCCUPATIONAL THERAPIST

Experts break problems into parts. The church organist told Cleven that he learned difficult music by taking it apart into pieces he could tackle one by one.

Music is kind of like ABCs. Step by step, you gonna have to catch the basics. The more letters you know, the more combinations and clusters you will be able to apply together to learn bigger words. It's the same with music! Harder musical pieces are like big words put into books. – CHURCH ORGANIST

Experts rely on evidence. Students noticed that the most accomplished people seek out evidence of which techniques result in success. Ever since Tacara's school basketball coach in Chicago had been a young player, he had made a habit of reviewing game tapes.

I used to get technical fouls all the time, because I felt like I couldn't do any wrong. When my coach showed me a game tape, I would pout at first. But seeing it on tape just really changed how I conducted myself on the court. – BASKETBALL COACH

Experts look for patterns. Using the information they had, the people whom students interviewed were always noticing patterns and making connections. The home beer-maker told Chelsea that he kept notes in a journal to help him figure out why the quality differed in each batch.

At the beginning I realized that all my off flavors were probably because of not keeping things spotless clean. Starting with freshly clean equipment, I noticed the beer was actually a lot better. You're always experimenting. I always put the date that I brewed the beer, but now I also keep track of the temperature. It has a lot to do with how your beer comes out. – BREWER

Experts consider other perspectives. These experts kept their minds open, students said. Alex, who studied theater at his California high school, spent a year writing a one-act play. When the time came to direct it, he found himself seeking guidance from visiting artists.

I have a really hard time looking at something that I've written with an outside eye. Does it really make sense, or is it only making sense to me because of the prior knowledge I have in my head? When you take the director's outside eye back into the piece, you understand it better. – ALEX

Experts follow hunches. When deciding what to do next about a problem, students noticed, these experts often seemed to trust their instincts. Perhaps through long experience they had learned to sort out the most promising possibilities. The Chicago police officer told Kelvin, for example, how he decides whether to act on his street-corner observations.

Suspicion and doubt come to my mind and something's not right. By looking at their body language, I can formulate questions to ask them. You see what their answers are, and if they're lying to you, then you know. – DETECTIVE

Experts use familiar ideas in new ways. Students saw a lot of creativity in how their experts approached a situation. They often would apply a familiar idea in an unconventional way. The tattoo artist whom Kristian interviewed, for example, tried a high-art technique on the human body.

I wanted to change the traditional-style tattoo with the bold outline colored in and bring in the realism style I was learning in college. I knew there had to be some way that I could put a painting on a person, make it look like a portrait, with no outlines. – TATTOO ARTIST

Experts collaborate. The Chicago police detective told Kelvin that he often shared his challenges with partners on his team.

The best advice I get is from the people I work with. You form a team of two or three guys and you ask to work with each other, because you know you can help each other. – DETECTIVE

Experts welcome critique. In Maine, Joe listened to a small farmer tell about his work in the fields. The man had learned his trade as an apprentice, he told Joe, and now he was training apprentices himself.

> It's not like you receive a set of instructions and the farmer goes off somewhere. It's very hands-on. The farmer you're working with is right there by your side, critiquing you: "Try holding your knife this way" or "Try weeding this way, it's a little bit better."
> — SMALL FARMER

Experts revise repeatedly. Zac asked his father to talk about his passion for making longboards in his free time. What most impressed him was his father's determination to keep working on a board until he had eliminated all its imperfections.

> He does it for fun. But he sees all the mistakes that nobody else sees, and he just can't take it when he messes up. To me it looks really good, but he just keeps on working on it. — ZAC

Experts persist. Kathryn's martial arts teacher, a master of the Kuk Sool tradition, had been practicing it for twenty-eight years. He told Kathryn about the endless rhythms of training with the monks in the mountains of Korea.

> You would do one thing thousands and thousands of times. You did not do it just for the sake of doing a passing thing, and then go on to this or that. It was an art form, a way of life. Your life depended on it. — MARTIAL ARTS MASTER

A vascular surgeon spoke to the Long Beach students about struggling his way through pre-medical courses at UCLA. When he got a D in genetics, he said, he almost gave up.

> I'm like, "Oh, man, I wanted to be a doctor and it doesn't look like it's going to happen." But then I went back and took that same

class again. I never worked harder than I did to get a B. Later I applied to medical schools, and I got fourteen rejections in a row. Again I thought, "I'm done." The fifteenth school was in Omaha and they said yes. Look, I don't do cold. I grew up in South Bay Los Angeles, not speaking English. But I said, "Hell, yes, I'm going to Omaha." You find it in yourself. – SURGEON

Experts seek out new challenges. We noticed that no matter how good they got at what they were doing, these people looked to stretch beyond it. They were always reaching to extend their grasp of what they knew and could do. For example, the Chicago teacher whom Andris interviewed spent her whole summer figuring out ways to work creative projects into her classroom.

It's almost a craving now; I really want to get better. I'm constantly thinking about school and what's going to be best for my students. A lot of times, waking up in the morning I'm dreaming about it.
– HIGH SCHOOL TEACHER

Experts know their own best work styles. As these accomplished practitioners worried away at what tested their limits, they did so, my students saw, in many different ways. Some would stay up all night thinking things through, and some needed to talk out ideas with others. Some of them worked better under pressure, and some needed a regular schedule of practice and production. All of them, however, seemed to know what they needed in order to achieve their best work—and they made sure they had those conditions.

Joey M. noticed this when he interviewed his uncle Anthony, who made his living in Chicago by repairing old record players. Self-taught since boyhood, his uncle had learned his trade by taking apart one old machine after another, trying to figure out how they worked. Early on he had established a rhythm of thinking things through, which he still counted on when tackling a perplexing repair.

The Habits of Experts

- ☐ Experts ask good questions.
- ☐ Experts break problems into parts.
- ☐ Experts rely on evidence.
- ☐ Experts look for patterns.
- ☐ Experts consider other perspectives.
- ☐ Experts follow hunches.
- ☐ Experts use familiar ideas in new ways.
- ☐ Experts collaborate.
- ☐ Experts welcome critique.
- ☐ Experts revise repeatedly.
- ☐ Experts persist.
- ☐ Experts seek out new challenges.
- ☐ Experts know their own best work styles.

Some pieces I would have a hard time figuring out, so I would just put it aside. Then I would go back to it and try to figure it out again. I would go back and forth, from one to the other. The more I did it, the more I would enjoy the challenge. Sometimes one would sit for six months. Then something would kinda be similar and, wait a min, it was like the old one that I put aside, so let me get that one. Okay, that's what it is: the A wire does not go with the B wire. That's when I knew I was getting better, because I could better identify the problem. — RECORD PLAYER REPAIRMAN

Like so many of the teenagers who did these interviews, Joey took what his uncle told him about his work and boiled it down to a principle of practice. "For him it was like a learning process over and over again," he said. "Like falling off a horse, you have to get back up."

Where Can Young People Talk to Experts?

Make an appointment for an interview. One or more students can contact an accomplished person to schedule a formal one-hour interview. Recording the interview with an audio or video recorder and then transcribing it helps students think better about what they learned.

Invite several experts to a group dialogue. A class, club, or youth group can identify three or four experts from different fields to join them for a discussion about their paths to excellence. Plan for at least two hours, and facilitate the discussion to balance adult and student voices. Refreshments can turn this into a special "power breakfast" or evening salon, but don't forget to take notes and reflect later on what the experts said.

Arrange student internships in the community. Schools with internship programs schedule regular time each week for students to volunteer at organizations in the community. The best such programs gather students in a weekly "internship seminar" to debrief and reflect on their experiences. In this setting, one discussion might center on their close observations of accomplished adults in the workplace.

Ask an employer. Many youth hold down paying jobs after school. If there are coworkers or supervisors whose work they admire, they might request an appointment to ask questions about their training and practice.

Talk with family and friends. Parents, grandparents, relatives, and neighbors may be highly accomplished at what they know and can do. Young people often find it easier to approach these familiar people for a recorded interview, and the adults involved are usually happy to oblige.

WHY ASK THE EXPERTS?

For most of these students, talking in depth with competent adults about their work was a new experience. They enjoyed asking these experts the same questions that I had asked them at the start of our work together: How did you get started? What was hard? What keeps you going? Who do you trust to tell you how you're doing? And they added their own question: Are you still getting better, and how?

In this stage of our project I also saw the students move into a new way of thinking about their own development of mastery. When they had talked with me earlier about the things they worked hard at, the kids mostly focused on simple descriptions of their experiences. But as they combed the adult interviews for evidence of habits that "the masters" shared, the kids also cast a more analytical eye on their own learning process. And though couched in very personal terms, their insights closely reflected the cognitive research in the field of expert development.

"I can see myself doing a lot of these things," said Ruben.

> With fixing cars, you can just go off on a hunch, like, "Oh, if I do this it will work." Over time you get more evidence of what works and you can say, "Well, if you don't do this like this, you're going to have problems." The more hands-on you do it, the more comfortable you feel with it. But no matter how much you think you know, you're going to do it in steps. Everything has to be done right or it's going to show later on. — RUBEN

Joey H., who had started archery at the age of six, thought back on ten years of close critique aimed at perfecting how he drew and released his bow.

> The key is not to learn bad habits, just because it's much harder to relearn than to learn the first time. — JOEY H.

Darrian, the young chess player from Brooklyn, recognized the mental habits of experts in how she worked out her moves.

> The answers aren't necessarily there. You have to actually figure it out, by recognizing patterns. You don't actually remember the exact positions you've seen before, just the ideas behind them. You're not combing through your memory, you're just looking at the board and thinking what you can do that's good at this particular moment. And then you associate it with something that you've seen before. — DARRIAN

Rosalie, whose passion was performing in musical theater, saw that she could not have expressed her creative talent if she had not first mastered the fundamental techniques of her art.

> The technique is your base, and you build off that base and kind of grow up through it into creativity. In your performance the technique is, like, muscle memory. — ROSALIE

And Joe, who interviewed the Maine farmer about his years of apprenticeship, compared that experience to his own schooling.

> The farmer had to go onto a farm where there were more-experienced farmers, and he just built off of that. In the classroom we already do that; the teachers are the masters and we are the apprentices, learning how to do things that they're good at. — JOE

Wherever such conversations with accomplished adults took place—in school, at home, or in the community—these young people gathered from them important new perspectives on what it took to do something really well. In our next chapter they dig down even deeper as we return to their own experiences to investigate the special role of *deliberate practice*.

CHAPTER FIVE

Exploring Deliberate Practice

S O FAR MY YOUNG collaborators were hearing the same
thing from everyone: that endless hours of practice went into an
expert's development, contributing
far more than innate talent did. Even
those who knew nothing about cognitive research—grandmothers who knit
or computer repair wizards—made
the same emphatic point. And no one
thought that ten thousand hours exag-
gerated the amount of time it took to
get really good at something.

> **WHAT KIDS TELL US**
>
> **Most of us don't really pay
> attention when we are
> watching someone else do
> something. It's better to
> make mistakes than to watch
> people do it the right way
> for you. You need to make
> mistakes to get better.**
>
> — BIANCA

But did all practice actually result in high performance? If
these teenagers banged away long enough at the drums, went to
enough play rehearsals, or conjugated enough verbs, would they all
turn into expert drummers, actors, linguists? We realized that sticking with it made a big difference—but we also suspected that effective practice had more to it than that.

So we decided to look together at what researchers in the development of expertise set forth as the criteria for *deliberate practice*—
that is, practice that gets the desired result of increasing mastery. By

holding up kids' practice sessions against these criteria, perhaps we would find out whether they were on the right track.

First, the students and I talked through a few things that researchers say *do not* count as such practice. The distinctions made sense to the kids on the basis of their own experiences.

- *Deliberate practice is not the same as work.* "When I'm fixing something on my car," said Ruben, "I might be doing my best, but I'm not exactly practicing a technique. I'm just trying to get the car repaired."

- *Deliberate practice is not the same as play.* "When I sit down with my guitar just for fun, I'm not necessarily trying to improve my technique or anything," said Marquis.

- *Deliberate practice is not the same as rote repetition.* All practice involves repetition, we would learn. But unless they cared about what they were repeating and why, students said, they were "doing it just to do it"—not to learn. "We have to memorize chemistry formulas for the test," said Christian. "But I never remember them later if I don't get what they're about."

ELEMENTS OF DELIBERATE PRACTICE

So what elements do qualify something as deliberate practice? Many researchers into cognition and learning, we found, describe it as follows:

- Practice has an express purpose.
- Practice demands attention and focus.
- Practice involves conscious repetition or rehearsal.
- Practice is geared to the individual.

- Practice takes careful timing.

- Practice is not inherently enjoyable.

- Practice develops new skills and knowledge.

- Practice applies to new endeavors.

As the students in Chapter Three told of keeping up their practice despite its difficulties, they showed us that deliberate practice also acts as a powerful motivating force. Doing their tasks with such intentionality, it seemed, turned their minds away from the tedious tick of the clock. With encouragement they learned to view practice as purposeful small steps that would eventually result in satisfying progress. In the next sections of this chapter, students examine the above criteria for deliberate practice and apply them one by one to their own experiences of working hard toward mastery.

Practice has an express purpose. Practice didn't get them anywhere, kids told me, unless they knew *why* they were doing it. If they could connect a practice activity to the larger picture, they were willing to push themselves harder to master it.

At fourteen, Darrian already ranked just a few points below "expert" in chess. But she remembered back in fifth grade, when she started beating better players in her Brooklyn school's chess club. Closely studying how each win came about helped her skills grow steadily, and by ninth grade she was playing for twelve hours every Saturday. Working with a chess tutor once a week for two hours, she would scrutinize the choices she made in tournaments.

> When you're playing, you write your games down in chess notation. Later the tutor will look at your games and tell you what you're doing wrong and how you can improve. It is very intensive, kind of like having a math tutor. – DARRIAN

During the school week, after she did her homework, Darrian spent an hour every day looking over other people's chess games in books.

> I replay them on the board, alone, and see how I could imitate them. I study different positions, aiming to learn more about different strategic ideas. Some of it is about memory, but most of it's about actually understanding it. I can memorize all the chess positions in the world and still be awful if I don't understand it. And I might never get that exact position—every position is different.
> — DARRIAN

Those hours of study paid off, Darrian said, every time she stared at her board in a tournament, looking for familiar patterns. For her the express purpose of this practice was to move into her long-term memory a fund of useful strategies that could help her win at her game.

No matter what the field, identifying a particular aim for practice made it more effective, these teenagers said. Chelsea, who was learning oratory, centered many a practice session on stamping out a particular undesirable speech habit.

> Inflection and pronunciation is definitely a huge part of speech delivery. I used to have a problem where I would click when making certain syllables. Every time I would do that in a sentence, my speech coach would make me start over from the beginning, until I weeded that out completely. I still say "like" a lot, and "umm," but my speech has to be memorized, so most of those get eliminated. But in everyday speech I think I've definitely cut down on that. — CHELSEA

Practice demands attention and focus.
Unless they paid close attention to what they were doing, students recognized, they did not get better at what they practiced. In practic-

ing the viola, said Joshua, he had to break down a daunting musical score and focus on one passage at a time.

> I used to think practicing was like, "Take out my music and just play through it, and then that's it." But if you practice the passage wrong, you have to work even harder to fix it. So now I'm learning how to practice the right way. My teacher has me pick a certain point where it's the hardest and play it the slowest I can without a mistake. Then I play the whole piece in that tempo. If I make the mistake again, I take that passage and work it little by little, and then he wants me to speed it up. — JOSHUA R.

For a science project involving DNA analysis of animal tissue, Tyler spent hours in the lab transferring samples from one test tube to another. He had to start over again and again because of frustrating mistakes, but he knew why the teacher insisted that students focus so closely on the procedure.

> You have to be very meticulous, because it's very easy to contaminate your samples. If you're not careful, when you finally go to sequence it, the DNA will come out as human. — TYLER

Patty, the softball player from New York City, needed to pay attention to every motion in a successful pitch when she was first learning the game. After enough practice, she said, throwing the ball across the plate started to come more naturally.

> Before throwing, you have to position yourself with a stable balance. Your feet are spread apart and you're able to move. After putting your glove on the other hand, you're ready to throw. You have to make an L shape with your arm and wind up slowly, making sure to hold the ball in a position that would send a ball down the middle. Throw it straight to your target, bringing your arm around. Then, if you made a mistake, you pick up the ball again and learn from it. — PATTY

Darrian said she could only remember chess moves if she tuned out all distractions.

> Most kids don't want to sit down for hours and try and solve a problem. But chess requires a lot of focus; you can't play a Gameboy, text, and watch TV while playing chess. You just have to sit there and do one thing. So I'm probably more capable of sitting down and thinking longer because I do it more. — DARRIAN

By giving their full attention to such tasks, these students were realizing, they laid down specific skills and knowledge in their brains to call on when they needed them later. Without that purposeful focus in their practice, they did not feel they were really getting better at something.

Practice involves conscious repetition or rehearsal. Whether they were trying to acquire information or practice a skill, doing something again and again made it stick in the minds of these students. Their experience matched what the research shows: without mindful repetition or rehearsal, learning just doesn't come back when we need it.

Christian, a student in our Long Beach group, enjoyed learning about the paintings in his Advanced Placement art history class, but he worried about identifying them all on the A.P. test. He set up conditions in which he knew he could concentrate, and then went over his "art cards" again and again.

> I wait until everybody's sleeping and I'm by myself at my desk, light on. I just focus on the card—the artist, the title, how it looks, symbols and everything—and try to repeat it, repeat it, repeat it. We have to know about forty cards, and I forget time—by the time I sleep, it's two A.M. or something. Next morning when I wake up, I go through the cards really easy. — CHRISTIAN

Such repeated tasks marked most of the endeavors in which my students had done exceptionally well. Whenever she had to give a speech in competition, Chelsea said, she rehearsed it "an insane amount of times."

> I practice two or three hours a week by myself, plus three practices with students and my coach. I usually put the speech in front of me and take it sentence by sentence. I say each sentence three times, and then start from the beginning and say everything I've memorized so far. Little by little, you'll memorize the entire thing that way. — CHELSEA

Kirby, who played with the community strings program in Providence, said her teachers made the repetitious nature of practice more appealing by offering endless ways for her to pick up her cello and play.

> We'll play fiddle lab for an hour, or have a class in improv music. Through giving us a variety of ways to practice, eventually you will get what you want, whether or not you practice getting that one note. They've taught us that if you get really comfortable with your instrument, you can basically get anything. — KIRBY

And by drawing his archer's bow in the right way time after time, Joey said, that physical motion lodged itself so deeply in his memory that it came back automatically when he needed it.

> You draw the bow and aim with your conscious mind, and then you're supposed to let your unconscious mind release it. Your muscles have memory; as you practice, they learn the motion, so your unconscious mind will do the work perfectly. — JOEY H.

Practice is geared to the individual. As we talked over their experiences, students concluded that effective practice depended on factors that varied with different people, different skills, and different points in the students' development.

In her gymnastics training, Rachel always spent the most time practicing the skills that she could do least well.

> My weakest event was the uneven bars and so I spent a majority of my time on that. I would have rather been on beam, which I loved doing because I was better at it, instead of constantly failing and having to do the same routine over and over again to try and perfect it. — RACHEL M.

Ariel, who had recently joined a skateboarding group in her New York high school, often had to try out several approaches before she could get the hang of a new technique.

> I learned by practicing over and over again. But it also matters how you do it, because there's multiple ways to do certain tricks. When our coach described how to do an ollie, I kind of didn't understand it and it seemed a lot harder. But then another skater showed me another way that worked better for me. It's basically experimental: just experiment with your feet and try to see which way is better for you. — ARIEL V.

Watching someone else do something well could show them what to aim for, students said. To make a skill their own, however, they had to practice it themselves.

> Most of us don't really pay attention when we are watching someone else do something. It's better to make mistakes than to watch people do it the right way for you. You need to make mistakes to get better. — BIANCA

Practice takes careful timing. Many students also had experience with another characteristic of deliberate practice: its timing also makes a difference. Focusing on his art cards just before bed every night, Christian said, seemed to help him recollect them best. And for an hour in the evening Darrian liked to study the chess games of other players. A good night's sleep seemed to help the information lodge in their memory, both of these students found.

Students who played music spoke of other patterns in timing their practice. Aaron, a trombone player from Long Beach, liked to practice in shorter and more frequent sessions. For him, picking up his horn often, even for brief periods, helped him in overcoming the difficulties of learning to play.

> I think it's better to practice five or ten minutes at a time, all day. When you get the practice done in a whole hour, throughout the day you're not thinking about it no more. It's like, "Okay, I've done my practice," and getting it out of the way. Then the next day I'll forget what I did—my brain starts messing up. But if you take ten minutes and then a break, and do that again and again, you're going to think about it more and more. It's going to rebuild into my mind, so I actually *get* what I've done. – AARON S.

Hunter, who was homeschooled in rural Maine until tenth grade, took up the banjo at the age of twelve. With the freedom to organize his days, for a couple of years he spent four hours a day picking banjo. Even so, Hunter said, at times he learned better after setting a tune aside for a while.

> A lot of the songs have a really strict melody. You can play all around it, but getting the melody perfect, it's real hard to know what you're doing. I would get aggravated with it and put it down for a week or so. It always seemed pretty easy to get the lick I was working on after that week. I just had to put it down and take a break from it. – HUNTER

Athletes as well often varied the timing of their practice to get the results they were looking for. Sometimes, for example, the best timing involved short bursts of intense exercise. Norbert, a Long Beach student who liked to work out, believed this method gave him the best results.

> It doesn't really depend on if you do it for hours. You can do it for five minutes, as long as you put all into it. Before I go to bed I practice pushups, stuff like that. And if you give it a hundred percent, and you sleep on it, muscle builds up. You get results.
> — NORBERT

Practice is not inherently enjoyable. My students often found practice intensely frustrating. Even if they really liked the thing they were working on, they always felt the strain of taking it to the next harder level. This characteristic too shows up in the criteria for deliberate practice: it is not necessarily enjoyable.

In Chicago, Patrick had to put in daily practice to build up his reading skills to the standard for eleventh grade. He kept his sessions short and looked for material that interested him, but his reading still felt laborious.

> I did not like reading for a long time, because it didn't really catch my attention. But you got to read at this school. So I started just reading ten to twenty minutes a day. When I started liking the books more, I got better, but I still have to really work at it. — PATRICK

Joe, who plays baritone sax in his Maine school's band, said it took willpower for him to keep practicing when he felt he was not doing well.

> You hit a sour note and you get frustrated. It starts to get into your head when you're messing up, and if you start telling yourself that you're not good at it, then you're going to eventually give up. You

have to remember that nobody really gets it at first—it takes a while to get the hang of it. – JOE

Ariel described her attempts to master new moves on the skateboard.

I get very agitated—especially if I did a trick one time by myself and I want to show other people but I can't get it again. It can be very upsetting and sometimes it discourages you. But you gotta keep practicing till you can get it down, every single time. – ARIEL V.

Hunter listened for hours to CDs of expert banjo players and tried to duplicate their sounds. Even after years of study it was painstaking and tedious work, he said.

You can hit the notes in three different spots on the neck of the banjo and it's extremely difficult to find the right area. I am still working on it now, trying to get it perfect. Also, it's a lot of work to remember over two hundred songs. You're just playing them over and over and over, until you get 'em. – HUNTER

All of these young people were aiming for the same thing: to make certain key knowledge and skills so familiar that they would come effortlessly when needed. As boring or difficult as their practice sessions sometimes felt, these kids had to believe they were heading in the right direction.

Practice develops new skills and knowledge. As their capacity increased, my young collaborators began to crave even more new knowledge and skills. This continual reaching for the next challenge, research indicates, separates experts from people who are merely "good enough."

By ninth grade, Darrian's years of practice had made her a formidable chess player. But she was always seeking out better players to sharpen her game.

When they make good moves, you also have to counter that with better moves—thinking harder, being more precise. When you have a really close position and you don't know what to do, or when you're losing, it's a frustration at that moment. But if the other player's position looks really nice, it's like reading a really good book: "Wow, how did they do that? That's amazing." You can't do that yet—but maybe one day you can. – DARRIAN

R. J., a high school senior from San Diego, saw the same thing when he played *Robot Wars* on his computer.

You build your own robot on your computer and then battle against each other, trying different strategies to be successful. It definitely involves mental work. Not everything works out the right way the first time; you have to continue and try and get better at it. – R. J.

Dan, who belonged to his eighth-grade ballroom dance team, told of how he put his own stamp on the techniques he was practicing.

To make it more fun for me, I always change something very slightly. I'll add a different feeling to a certain step, so even though it's the same step and you're practicing it the same way, there's this different emotion to it, which makes the process more interesting. You never stay at something; there's always something that you could approach differently. – DAN

Alex, who worked in the student-run theater at his California school, said that his practice in the dramatic arts was changing how he approached all learning.

Theater has this intense emphasis on comprehension. You have to understand what you're saying, the circumstances in which you are saying it, the person you are saying it to, your relationship to that person. All these different aspects carry over with me to everything else that I'm doing. I'm not okay anymore, just "kinda, sorta" knowing. There's this thing in the back of my head saying I need to understand *why*. – ALEX

Practice applies to new endeavors. "Basically, you just have to find something that makes you want to do good at all those other things," remarked Jo'Nella, a tenth grader in Harlem. By building strong habits of practice in their favorite activities, these young people concluded, they were steadily gaining strength and confidence that helped them with difficult tasks in other contexts.

Rodrigo, a violinist in his school orchestra, had recently been thinking of engineering as a possible career. "Music is not much different than engineering," he said.

> It's the same concept. It's creation. With violin you have to get the technical stuff down, and once you have that it's like, "Okay, let's make it more interesting." Engineering, you have all these pieces in a pile and then you're like, "Let's see what we can make out of it." – RODRIGO

Henry, an aspiring chef at thirteen, said he enjoyed science more because it reminded him of cooking.

> Cooking is chemistry and you need to add the right ingredients, same as you do in science when you're making chemicals. If you screw up in chemistry then it's like screwing up in cooking—it can all go wrong or you can create a fire. So when we do experiments I really do learn how I can improve my cooking. – HENRY

Even basketball, Aaron noticed, had something in common with academic disciplines. To do well, he had to understand *why* he was playing by the rules of the game.

> Once you understand the reason for those rules—the concepts behind what you're doing—it makes it more exciting. You enjoy

the game a whole lot more, and you start to improve. That's what puts you in that mind-set that focuses you, where this is the thing that matters. — AARON S.

Other students also noticed that practicing outside activities sharpened their mental habits. Janiy, for example, thought her music training was changing her.

Playing the piano, being interested in music, it can help you to become more precise. It'll help you with your exactitude. It makes your senses sharper. — JANIY

Some students commented on the self-knowledge and maturity they had gained through confronting new challenges on a regular basis. For a year Luke had spent all his spare time in the family garage converting a gas-powered car to run on electricity. When problems came up, he said, he learned to rely on his own initiative.

My dad would give me advice on certain things. But he had a business to run, so I couldn't interrupt and ask him all these questions about how currents ran and everything. So if I didn't understand something or ran into a problem, I just looked at the schematic harder and tried to figure it out for myself, by trial and error. — LUKE

As students gained strength through practice in situations like these, they felt themselves growing more capable of managing their lives, dealing with interpersonal tensions, and rising to the occasion in many other contexts. Joe, who had been out looking for a paying job, remarked on the personal discipline it required of him.

I'm just kind of being thrown out there, because my parents are making me pay for my car and insurance and the things regular people have to take care of. I have to learn how to maintain an interview and how to manage my time. You can't succeed in work and not in school, because then you won't advance farther. But you can't succeed in school and not in work, because then you'll get fired. – JOE

For each new time they mastered something hard, these students saw changes in the way they approached their other work. "See, that's the way I do my life now," said Joshua, the viola player from Providence.

I kinda do piece by piece. I don't try to overwhelm myself all at once. Don't wait until the last moment every single day, then have all the stuff together and run through all of it. I used to do that. Now I just take it and work little by little on each one, on this day and that day and that day, and I'll make good progress. – JOSHUA R.

TAKING PRACTICE FORWARD

By now these teenagers had constructed a clear picture of what they were doing when they deliberately practiced the things they cared about. They had analyzed the demands and the difficulties of that practice, and they could see its results emerging as their own abilities grew. No matter where they decided to invest their energies, they had a new understanding of how to go about it.

The students' interviews with the experts, discussed in Chapter Four, had also left them with a new sense of themselves. They recognized their own experiences in the learning process that accomplished practitioners described. And they sensed that—even in their teens—they already had a place in the community of expertise. In the next chapter, we explore what it means to young learners to demonstrate their growing mastery even as they continue to develop it.

CHAPTER SIX

Practice and Performance

A T THIS POINT, MY teenage co-investigators had a very good handle on what made them want to learn to do something well. They had come to terms with the nature of deliberate practice—its requirements and its seemingly endless toil. They saw that even the people they thought of as experts were always learning more and reaching for greater challenges.

Increasingly these young people felt included in the community of those who valued real mastery—and they wanted to exercise their growing strengths in every way they could. As they came to realize that expertise was a *process*, not a *product*, the line between practice and performance grew less important to them. By using what they knew and could do, these students saw, they would only grow better at it.

Just how to do that, however, was a different question. Looking back on their own experiences as well as on their expert interviews, we noticed that opportunities to perform knowledge and skills took many different forms:

- *Some people perform for an audience.* "Theater is about human interaction," said Rachel C. about performing in her school's drama program. "You could do the most fabulous monologue ever—but without an audience, it won't matter."

- *Some people apply their mastery on the job.* "We're going to use bacteria to clean up the water quality in the San Diego Bay," said Jewel, who worked as a student intern in a naval research laboratory. "I like knowing how much our work will contribute to other things."

- *For some, mastery simply yields private satisfaction.* "Sometimes you get to that point of focus and you didn't even know," said Christian, the student who learned to love great paintings in his art history class. "You start working even better, and at one point you're like, 'Wait, wow, I was just in tune, like second nature.'"

We could probably use the word *performance* for all these different uses of someone's expertise, my students and I decided. Point by point we looked into each example.

PERFORMING BEFORE AN AUDIENCE

Whether they felt excited or apprehensive at the prospect of performing before an audience, students agreed that it raised the stakes. Moira, a San Antonio student, explained:

> It's a personal expression you're conveying to the world. You put yourself out there, so it's more important to you. Even if you love what you're doing, it's still difficult, because inherently we're vulnerable. — MOIRA

Hunter spent endless hours playing along with CDs of expert banjo pickers before he got up his nerve to join in with the experts at bluegrass festivals.

The first time you play with other people, there is a huge difference compared to playing along with a CD. It takes building up your confidence. I never like kicking off a song when I'm playing with people, because that sets the tempo and the beat for the singers. They are all relying on you to get it right so they can sing the song the way they are comfortable with it. Once you kick them off, you get more confidence. — HUNTER

Deepika took up classical Indian dance when she was a young girl, to connect with her family's heritage. In high school she pushed herself hard to prepare for a trip to India that would include performing before an especially discerning audience.

I can't mess up. I have to do my expressions right, depict the right cultural aspects and religious stories—everything perfect. So I now have a purpose for practicing more regularly and in the right way: stretching my arms out, having the right posture, expressing the right things. It gives me a thrill to go on stage and perform. It's something that I'm working towards. — DEEPIKA

Many students said that connecting with an audience helped them infuse a creative fire into their skills, lifting them from ordinary to exceptional. Rachel M., a former gymnast, explained:

At a lower level, all the competitors do the same exact compulsory routines—the same music, same movements—and the judges assess based on objective comparisons. But you start to see expert gymnasts enhance the routine. They do the same exact motions somebody else might do, but they might do it with more life.
— RACHEL M.

However, competitive performances also raised the pressure on them, others observed. Darrian, our young chess player from Brooklyn, described her state of mind in tournament play.

> Normally people aren't happy when they're playing chess. It's not a
> social feeling. It's not adrenaline, pumped up and excited. It's a
> feeling of playing: just me and my brain, staring, to find a good
> move. Chess isn't something that you get by luck. You have to
> think about every single thing. There's never a moment where it's
> just, "Relax." Chess is like a duel. But no one panics. — DARRIAN

Amauri, a soccer player from San Antonio, felt that same demand for
both strategy and ingenuity in his high-stakes matches.

> I think every player has to have a sense of creativity in order to win
> in soccer. Once you get high up in the field, it gets a lot tighter in
> the defense. So you have to know how to get open for a player. You
> have to have vision, you have to know what you are going to do in
> order to score. — AMAURI

To perform in public, said Dan, an aspiring actor, he had to call
up on the spot what he knew and could do. Yet it also taught him
things he did not learn in any other way, he said. In that sense, it was
another kind of practice.

> When you're in a show, each performance is practice for the next
> show. You're learning from it, but yet you're treating it as a per-
> formance as well. — DAN

APPLYING MASTERY ON THE JOB

People could also be "performing" their expertise without explicitly
presenting their work to an audience, these teenagers believed. Their
best teachers did that every day, they agreed. And students could
think of many other experts who applied their knowledge and skills
to solve complex problems in their fields.

One group of students had interviewed a surgeon, who said he
treated each case as a new challenge to be solved. Several Maine

When Are We Ready to Perform for an Audience?

Is there a particular point when students are ready to "perform" for an audience? Who decides, and on the basis of what criteria? From students' experiences, we came up with these examples of when to "go public":

- ☐ When we have reached a milestone in our learning
- ☐ When we think we are ready to make our learning public
- ☐ When our teacher or coach thinks we are ready to make our learning public
- ☐ On a set schedule, so we are always working toward a performance
- ☐ When someone has need of what we know and can do

teenagers had interviewed local farmers, who continually looked for new ways to improve the quality of their crops or herds. Joey's uncle in Chicago and Ruben's father in San Antonio had spoken with obvious pride about solving baffling problems in the machines that people brought them.

At R. J.'s San Diego school, engineers from the local high-tech community mentored the student robotics club. He saw them as models of the ways in which experts keep looking for new problems to solve.

> Engineering is all they think about. They've just practiced it to the point where it does almost come naturally to them. It's really neat to be a part of it. — R. J.

These people, we agreed, demonstrated their expertise in what we could call a "practice": a teaching practice, a medical practice, a working farm, or a shop where they practiced a craft or trade. Simultaneously, they were continually striving to get better, rising on the scale of how well they performed in their fields.

Most of my student collaborators were not at the stage of mastery where they had a working "practice" themselves. But our earlier inquiry had already established that age did not stand in the way of expert status. Almost all of us knew a "go-to" kid who could work around a tricky computer problem, or interpret between two languages, or braid hair like a pro. And although the rest of the crowd might not be at that level, many teenagers were in the early stages of pursuing an interest that could result someday in a working practice.

For example, as a high school student in San Antonio, Rachel M. had an interest in social and political activism. For her senior year internship, she decided she would organize a monthly nonprofit café at her church to raise money for a medical mission in Vietnam. She undertook the project on her own, getting advice from the church's youth director.

> At the beginning it was really stressful. I was always trying to figure out the best way of doing things: the sound for the band, decorations and chairs, all the food, organizing the volunteers. And once I got to a certain point I was like, "Okay. I think I got this. I can do this again." — RACHEL M.

As her organizing skills and knowledge increased, Rachel looked for more ways to use them for the good of others. She volunteered for the local campaign headquarters in the presidential race, stretching her capacities even further and building new strengths.

> It really took a lot of research on my part. I had to be able to say, "I believe in this and this and this, and this is why." That was hard. And more so than ever in my life, I had to learn to work with other people of so many different cultures. — RACHEL M.

As other students told similar stories of pushing themselves to develop, we began to notice an interesting pattern. The ones who felt they were climbing the ladder of expertise invariably were engaging in what we could call performance—real-world, hands-on, and often public applications of their developing knowledge and skills.

By the age of thirteen, Henry was already a regular volunteer at a yearly cooking exposition in New York City. He aspired to study culinary arts and he loved to put on a white uniform and assist the master chefs.

> The chef's out front showing everyone how to make the stuff, and we're preparing all kinds of samples backstage. Sometimes I go up on stage with one of the chefs and help them stir it, or if there's something that they need for their presentations, I run in the back and get it. – HENRY

For an extended school project, Tyler had the chance to work with scientists at a San Diego laboratory.

> You don't want to mess up in front of them, so you're constantly trying to prove yourself. It's not so much a status thing as it is "This person knows a lot and is very important. I don't want to mess up what they are doing." It's so easy to contaminate a sample or add the wrong amount of a chemical that you have to make sure everything is just right before you do it. – TYLER

Performing such tasks in the field, these students said, made them realize the value of their earlier practice. Just as with an actor on the stage, they felt that every new performance brought them further toward expertise.

PERFORMING FOR ONESELF

Could we describe people as "performing" if they were acting in solitude, for their own pleasure or satisfaction? The students and I found it hard to decide. But they could describe many solo situations that they believed went beyond deliberate practice and should count as performance.

Dan, for example, told of his satisfaction at solving puzzles on his own.

> When you're solving those Sudoku games, it's something to both relax you and make you overcome something. And you feel proud of yourself when you do it. — DAN

For Christina, learning the guitar opened her to a world of solitary pleasures.

> When you learn how to play an instrument, not only do you accomplish it, but then in time you get to put your own feeling into it and make your own stuff. If you feel really depressed or happy, you can write your own music. — CHRISTINA

Even with an audience, these students said, their satisfaction felt more private than public. Dylan noted that in a race he often ran for the sheer contentment that it gave him.

> It's not one of those things that I want to "get done"—it's the process of it. The strategy, the other runners around you, everything going through your head—I love that sort of thing. I'll be happy with myself after completing a race. — DYLAN

EXPERIENCING FLOW

Not quite work, not quite play, many of these varied performance activities put my students in a state of "flow": utter absorption in a challenging task that was just within their powers. Skateboarding on his own, Andrew said, could send him into a state of perfect focus and fulfillment.

I'm just concentrating on what I have to do. Like, you're not even paying attention to anything else. If you're on a roll, if you're landing everything, you're not even noticing that something else is happening. You don't even notice time flying by. You're heading to school and you're doing these tricks that's really good and you don't want to stop—until you notice you're late for school. – ANDREW

Students also told of experiencing flow when they were publicly performing or competing, or when they were working as a team. Darrian said she feels it in a challenging chess game.

I'm kind of in a chess zone. You don't talk. It's really mellow and quiet, just sitting there for hours and hours, thinking. Me and the board and that's it. It's like everything just goes away. I'm not aware of what's going on around me. Someone could walk by and I don't even know that they're there. Music, I don't hear it. Hunger, it all goes away. It's just calmness—me thinking and winning.
– DARRIAN

Kenzie described a soccer game with teammates who had played together for years.

We've communicated for years and gotten to know each other's styles, so we relay to each other, like a fluid motion, our ideas about the game and what we're going to do. You tell someone, even if it's not by speaking, that you're going to this place and be in this position. – KENZIE

In the details of their most authentic learning experiences, my students had now identified the key elements of "what it takes to get really good at something": where they had started, what kept them going, how they practiced, and what it meant to perform. It was time to turn our gaze more directly onto the world of the classroom, looking at it too through the lens of practice.

CHAPTER SEVEN

Bringing Practice into the Classroom

T HESE TEENAGERS AND I had a new respect, at this point, for what it took to get really good at something. In the areas where they truly had an interest, they were putting in hours of deliberate practice—following the same process and building the same habits that experts use.

We all saw the problem, however. All too often that powerful engagement was happening largely in young people's outside activities: arts, athlet-

WHAT KIDS TELL US

If I just sit there like a rock and don't actively participate, then I won't remember anything from it. But when I'm required to do something with my hands or with my body, I seem to remember it better.

— JOE

ics, hobbies, games. When it came to academic knowledge and skills—the reading, writing, history, foreign languages, science, and math that citizens need in a democracy—their schooling seldom generated a comparable drive for mastery.

The classroom, kids agreed, should also be a place where they are always practicing things that have meaning and importance. They wanted school to introduce them to new interests and exciting exemplars from the world of ideas in action. They hoped for adult guides who knew their strengths and believed in their potential. Expertise in academic subjects would require many more years of study, my students knew. But during our Practice Project they had come to see their mastery as something dynamic and ongoing, involving individuals and families but also communities and institutions. It flowed from what kids already valued and from their opportunities to try new things. It thrived on their close relationships and on practice sessions tailored just for them. Its rewards came from within and from the recognition and respect of others.

We realized that whatever motivation young people felt—as well as the all-absorbing sense of flow that accompanied their most intensive practice—came as a *result*, not a predecessor, of all these factors. What would it take to bring that same excitement and flow into the classroom experience?

GETTING STARTED

As we've seen again and again, relationships and opportunities, far more than innate talent, first drew these young people into the outside activities that engaged them most. Someone important to them offered a chance to explore something together. That could also happen in school, kids said, if adults opened the door.

Curriculum did not have to correspond with their existing interests in order to draw them in, they noted. Many kids, in fact, got started on something because they just wanted to be around someone who cared. Whether knitting or history, the interest often followed the relationship, not the other way around.

> A lot of the teachers here treat their class as more of a conversation, rather than a lecture, and I think that really helps to create dialogue. There's not someone standing up and telling you a right or wrong answer. — KRISTIAN

A lot of times I didn't like to talk or answer questions, because I was afraid of sounding stupid. But she would never let you just sit and observe. She always wanted you in the conversation. She would make you talk, but not in a mean way, in a really encouraging way, like, "Hey, Erika, what do you think about this?" and then if I said a quick answer, "Can you elaborate on that?" It made me feel like my thoughts were valid. — ERIKA

Sometimes teachers brought academic topics to life by building emotional connections to the material, students said. A story, a conflict, a puzzle, a compelling question, an association with a person or a goal—all could attach meaning and importance to material introduced in class.

Any field has something interesting about it, so tell us! If it really is that important, you can start by saying, "Look how interesting this is," and ask us to think about "Why is this? Where does this come from?" — NICK

Aaron failed science two years in a row at his Long Beach high school before a teacher helped him engage with the work in that way.

They would just throw out the material to us, not really explain it, so I kind of hated it. I never understood why we have a moon or why we orbit around the sun. And now my teacher really breaks down why certain things happen. We have a moon because there was a large asteroid that ran into earth and broke off and orbited around the earth. I never knew that before this year! I love that type of science. It makes me want to learn more and more about it, to understand the concept. I get on the computer looking at why volcanoes erupt and why we have hurricanes and tornadoes. I go to the library and study on it, or I go ask my dad. We'll sit down for forty-five minutes and then spend four hours talking about it. — AARON S.

Much of what these adolescents learned on their own time, we've seen, started when they were with their friends. In school, doing something fun with peers could also jump-start learning. Chelsea's science teacher, for example, got the class to its feet to learn the basics of biology.

> He'd have us all stand up and pretend to be molecules, like actually act out what their jobs are—cell organelles, nucleus and mitochondria, and stuff like that. That definitely stuck in my head.
> — CHELSEA

A small-group drama exercise helped Iona get into reading literature.

> We had to work in groups and put on a play for the class. Everyone in the group had to contribute something to the play and work cohesively. I'm not that great of an actress but I enjoyed it, even though I was a little shy. It came out great. — IONA

For her middle school art class, Bianca explored a new art form with her friend.

> We chose to take a picture together of our faces and make a mosaic. It was a very long process and we were so new at it that we learned more than just making a mosaic. After a while we got the hang of it and it was really fun. Once we got really good at it, our teacher took us to a museum to look at mosaics and we were fascinated with them. — BIANCA

COACHING US THROUGH DELIBERATE PRACTICE

Once drawn into a challenge in school, my students said they kept at it willingly—if their teachers coached them through the kind of deliberate practice that helped them move ahead in other areas, such as athletics and the arts. We looked again at what that practice should entail, this time taking the viewpoint of the classroom learner.

Let us see what we're aiming for. Kids told in Chapter Three of gaining inspiration and motivation by seeing examples of "best work" in their fields. In the classroom, studying exemplary work by others also boosted their determination to stick out the hard parts and do well.

When a first-rate work sample came from another student, it sometimes appealed to the others' competitive impulses. "I totally do better when I have somebody to compete with on my work," said Brandie. Even those students who felt differently said that the good work of peers gave them more confidence that they could rise to the same level.

Often students' interest increased when they engaged with "real-world" uses of academic knowledge. Jewel found the study of genetics very demanding. But she knew why she was doing it, she said.

> You could really see how it applies to people—how genes are passed on and things like that. I want to be a doctor and that just kept me going. If something like that makes you excited, you're going to want to keep doing it even though it's hard. — JEWEL

At the start of a unit on geology, Kenzie's science teacher proposed a midterm trip to study the rock strata in a nearby nature area.

> In order for us to really get anything out of the trip, we'd need this base of knowledge, so we'd have to be prepared. That gave us a reason to help each other learn the knowledge in the subject area. — KENZIE

Break down what we need to learn. These teenagers already knew that their skills in extracurricular activities did not develop all at once. To keep up their best efforts at school too, they needed to take it step by step. They wanted classroom teachers to act as outside coaches do: first helping them identify the knowledge and skills they needed, then setting realistic goals that they could achieve if they tried.

When You Are Learning Something New

An exercise for teachers

Think back to a time when you were learning something new. What were you learning? (It can be academic or nonacademic, work-related or fun, athletic or artistic or practical.)

_____

_____

People can learn things in lots of different ways. In this situation, what worked for you? Check off all that apply, or add your own description.

- ☐ I listened to a lecture.
- ☐ I watched a demonstration.
- ☐ I read a written description.
- ☐ I looked at pictures of someone doing it.
- ☐ I tried a few things on my own until I got it.
- ☐ Someone coached me one-on-one.

Memories and reflections:

_____

_____

After the first time, did you . . .

- ☐ Practice on your own?
- ☐ Practice in a group?
- ☐ Practice with one other learner?
- ☐ Practice with a coach present?

Memories and reflections:

_____

_____

◆ NOTE: *To download this worksheet as a pdf, please go to www.firesinthemind.org*

What kind of practice helped you most?

- ☐ Small amounts of practice several times a day
- ☐ A longer period of practice once a day
- ☐ Longer periods, but not every day

Memories and reflections

_____

_____

When you became discouraged, what motivated you to continue? (Check all that apply.)

- ☐ An upcoming performance
- ☐ An upcoming competition
- ☐ The positive expectations of someone else (teacher, parent, coach)
- ☐ The negative expectations of someone else
- ☐ Your career goals (money, fame)
- ☐ The satisfaction of knowing or doing something well

Memories and reflections:

_____

_____

If you are in a group with others, share what you remembered.

- Did you all have the same responses?
- If not, how did they differ?
- Whose learning needs were not met, and why?
- In a classroom of students with different needs, how can you ensure that they are practicing in a way that works for them?
- Memories and reflections

_____

_____

A learning task worked best for kids if the teacher broke it down into chunks, then assigned just the practice that a student was ready for. If they could not expect to succeed, their motivation shriveled and died.

Kristian had always loved to draw, for example, but when she finally took art classes in high school, she felt discouraged and mortified at all she did not know.

> People were expecting me to do things that I had never learned. It was really difficult for me, like, "What's the point of trying if I don't know how to do this stuff?" – KRISTIAN

In contrast, Christian's math teacher first helped him connect with the meaning behind a problem, then outlined the steps he might use to solve it.

> If I don't understand the concept, I can't understand the problem. But what if I don't know the steps to solve it? I have to focus myself on the concept and the steps together. I'll see the teacher do some problem on the board, and I try to move the same steps to a different problem that has the same concept. – CHRISTIAN

Give us lots of ways to understand. Deliberate practice must be geared to the individual, students had learned by now. To understand and remember something, they needed to encounter it in a form that their own brains could easily take in.

> I learn by doing. It's very crucial for me to learn through my body. In a class, if I just sit there like a rock and don't actively participate, then I won't remember anything from it. But when I'm required to do something with my hands or with my body, I seem to remember it better. – JOE

Presenting a concept in different ways—visual, tactile, aural—helped kids find their foothold. Brandie's math teacher had the ideal approach, she said.

He tries to do it different for different people. He draws diagrams on the board and he also writes it in words. He'll put you in groups of four and he'll walk around the whole time and see what people are doing. That's helpful because he knows if you get it, and he's really comfortable to talk to if you need help. – BRANDIE

Tessa told how her science teacher introduced difficult material about electromagnetic waves in a unit on astronomy.

He put this big yellow ball as the sun, and he made some people get up and demonstrate the different movements of the waves. When you saw the people doing it, you could kind of see, and then he had a word trick to make you remember what they were doing and how that connected to the radio waves. And that helped me learn it. – TESSA

Teach us to critique and revise everything we do. Deliberate practice involves close attention at every step of the task and repeated attempts to get it right. Kids knew this from such efforts as learning to cook or to dance, where they repeatedly went back to what they were doing, looking at it with a critical eye.

At school, Erika said, students also needed time to revise their work.

You get back a paper and maybe you didn't do so well on it. But the teacher will explain to you why and you'll have the opportunity to redo it and turn it in and improve your grade. So it makes grades less important—it's more about learning to fix your mistakes. – ERIKA

In the beginning, revising was frustrating, said Ninoshka, a tenth grader in New York. But as the product started to look better, she began to resee and rethink her work.

At first I kept messing up. But then after a while it gets better, and you feel happy that you've learned it. So then you want to start over

so it will look better at the beginning. It's looking like something, and then you feel that you can keep on doing it and learn more.
— NINOSHKA

When a teacher coached students to critique each other's work in a constructive manner, it helped them develop a culture of excellence in which everyone played a part.

> It's a practice thing—making sure that students are comfortable enough with each other to share things with each other, once a thing is accomplished. The critique starts with a positive thing, and then we go into, "Here's my advice for you to improve." It's not tension. We've built that trust already. — DENISE T.

Assess us all the time, not just in high-stakes ways. Like a good coach, an expert teacher was always watching students for signs of progress or difficulty in their understanding. Building in small "performances"—where students explained an idea briefly to others, or summarized in a paragraph what they understand, or even took an ungraded pop quiz—gave both teacher and students a good sense of where they needed help.

Joe's math teacher often asked students to write out their thinking about how to solve a problem. Joe didn't enjoy doing it, but he was starting to understand why it helped a teacher give him just the type of coaching he needed.

> From the standpoint of a teacher, I'd really want to see how that person got there—to understand how their mind works and how they work through problems. — JOE

When kids were reluctant to reveal their uncertainty, however, teachers often missed it altogether.

> Sometimes teachers make you raise your hand and do a "1-2-3-4-5"—how many fingers, how well are you getting this? But in

math class I sometimes do a 3 or 4 even though I didn't get any of it, because I don't want to feel really stupid when everybody else has 4s and 5s. – BRANDIE

Chart our small successes. Satisfaction at doing something well—even if it was a small step—made all these students want to keep going. The musicians among them felt new confidence when they mastered the first section of a new piece, and so did the runners when they beat their "personal best" time. Kids hoped that academic teachers, like their best coaches, would chart and celebrate their progress along the way.

Some teachers invited students to document their own journey to mastery by keeping track of personal goals with the help of simple rubrics framed in terms of "doing" verbs (such as *organize, predict, defend, explain,* or *illustrate*). The more they took ownership of the particular tasks they wanted to master, the more their motivation increased. As with activities outside school, they often worked hard at a challenge just for the satisfaction of proving that they could meet it.

A teacher's encouragement and pride along the way made a big difference, these students said. As Marquis was learning Japanese, for example, his teacher's belief in his growing skill was contagious.

Somebody's helping you all the way, inch by inch. You see that, "Hey, three months ago I couldn't do what I'm doing now; let me see what I can do in another three months." And you keep pushing yourself. – MARQUIS

Ask us to work as an expert team. In sports, music, and the workplace, kids noted, people didn't have to excel at every aspect of a task in order to create a successful outcome for their team. Classroom learning should work the same way, they said, with students relying on each other. Rachel's math teacher expected students to work out problems together, with him as a coach on the side.

He'll walk around to the tables, and so we're all working together in groups, trying to figure out these problems. And as he's walking by he'll just observe what we're doing, and if we have a question we can ask him. Or he'll just give us encouragement and say, "you're on the right track." So eventually we figure it out. – RACHEL M.

Joe's biology teacher created groups of five or six students to learn about cell theory.

This person has mitochondria, this person has the motor protein, this person has the Golgi apparatus, and we're supposed to know as much as we can about that one organelle and then share it to the group. It gets done a lot quicker, and since the students are teaching, it feels like we can relate. – JOE

Just as the social elements of learning could jump-start students' interest in a topic, so deliberate practice as a group often took kids farther than they might go on their own. Along the way they were developing their skills in teamwork and collaboration, a subject we explore further in Chapter Nine.

Help us extend our knowledge through using it. Deliberate practice leads to new knowledge and skills, which then opens the door to even more. The trick to opening that door, kids speculated, was to somehow put their new knowledge and skills to use. A teacher could explain the rules of chess, for example, but they learned the game only by playing it.

To Luke, calculus felt disconnected. To understand it, he had to apply it to some situation in the world.

If it was more interactive, not just the teacher standing up there and giving a lecture, I probably would still be understanding. I needed a way to follow along that kept me involved and didn't

lose me, and actual work to do in class, not worksheets. Eventually
I just stopped trying to do it. – LUKE

Dylan learned much more science doing lab experiments, he said,
than he did from teachers lecturing to the class.

I've always learned better that way than with a teacher at the front
of the class teaching us random facts about different types of
chemicals. Doing the experiment myself and seeing the results
helped me learn those things easier and to remember everything
about them. – DYLAN

When they had the chance to apply academic learning in authentic ways that mattered to them, my students agreed that nothing else
came close. They say more about that in Chapter Nine, where they
describe the project-based learning that most engaged them in school.

GIVE US AN AUDIENCE

In life outside school, as students said in Chapter Five, they kept practicing something mostly because they knew they would have to perform it. Whether that performance took the form of a baseball game, a
concert, a car that needed fixing, or a web site to launch, it asked them
to *show* what they knew and could do. In school as well, anticipating a
demonstration of their knowledge and skills helped students see academic practice in a new light. Just as with outside activities, they said,
preparing for such a performance should include many smaller steps.

Use performances to assess our academic understanding. Something
about performing raised the stakes, students said, wherever it took
place. At the end of an academic unit or year, having to show others
what they knew lent urgency, excitement, and meaning to all the
practice that went into their work.

Ruben found performance-based assessments far more motivating than tests.

> You don't want to look like a fool while you're up there in front of people trying to do something serious. You try to do more so you'll look like you know what you're talking about and people will respect you. With a test or writing a paper, people won't be so interested. If you pass it, then, okay, you're going to get a grade. It's not like you really need to push yourself to go beyond what's going to be on the test. — RUBEN

Because performance required continual rehearsal, critique, and revision, it helped these students build more authentic understanding and mastery that lasted. For tests, Bridget said, she did not push herself that far.

> Usually with a test you get to take it only once, and you're only tested by one person. With a presentation, though, it's not just the teacher who's gonna be disappointed in you; it's gonna be a whole audience. You have your peers judging you, and outside people, so you want to present the best of yourself. And that pressure creates a better product. — BRIDGET

Avelina remembered a group project for English class in which students reenacted a book as one of her best efforts ever in the classroom. Its assessment, she said, brought many hours of practice to an exciting and meaningful climax.

> It was very interesting, it took a lot of time, and the group I worked with put so much effort into it. The end result was amazing—even our science teacher came up and saw it. It felt so great being able to show our class what really interested us. That driving force made us do everything we could to make it the best. — AVELINA

PLANNING FOR PRACTICE IN CLASS

The most boring material students had in class, they told me, was often directly linked to high-stakes standardized tests they would be taking. Kids could tell that their teachers worried about tilting the balance toward fun activities at the expense of "rigorous" material that might be on the test.

However, my students said, even information that at first seemed dry and boring could stick in their memory with the right kind of practice. To demonstrate that, we decided to take a common test topic and think up a practice-based unit that would cover all the material they should have to know. The sidebars that follow in the next few pages all come from our research and discussions about that challenge, which so many teachers face as they plan their curriculum, instruction, and assessments.

How could a teacher draw students into the topic at the start, sparking their willingness to engage with it? What kind of practice should kids carry out so they would recall important material long after passing the test? What more engaging form of assessment could also ensure they had really mastered the facts and could put them to use?

For our sample unit, we chose the American Revolution, because students agreed that it was important to know, and because it presented perspectives, events, names, dates, places, and other information that they found difficult to recall—and that often showed up on tests. Then, for the chart on page 113, we brainstormed curriculum approaches that we thought would achieve rigorous academic learning—through deliberate practice that also drew students in.

Knowing about the American Revolution, these students recognized, did matter to their lives as educated citizens in a democracy.

They actually looked forward to the chance to learn about it, as long as that learning came alive through this kind of practice. And they could think of many other topics that would either bore or engage them—depending on how the teacher drew them into the topic, how they practiced the knowledge and skills required, and how they demonstrated their level of mastery.

In what specific areas did teachers think students needed more practice? Could teachers use the same chart to come up with interesting practice in other potentially boring topics? For example:

- Factoring a quadratic equation
- Understanding the laws of thermodynamics
- Knowing the elements of the periodic table
- Analyzing a Shakespeare soliloquy or sonnet
- Knowing verb conjugations in a foreign language
- Writing a persuasive essay
- Researching a civic issue

These students agreed that participating in the conversation about classroom practice gave them new energy and interest in the work itself. Why not draw kids into such planning more often, to strengthen the purpose and value of their practice? For example, many students wanted to come up with their own series of realistic mastery goals, tailored to their individual learning needs. The teacher would provide consistent feedback as they demonstrated progress and would recognize each success along the way.

As one way to organize that conversation, no matter what the learning topic was, we devised the worksheet on page 114 and the checklist on pages 115–116.

Practicing Toward Mastery

Students' suggestions for learning about the American Revolution

You want us to know . . .	Important perspectives, events, names, dates, places, and other information about the American Revolution
You catch our interest by . . .	Role-playing in class the Revolution's important events, introducing their main characters and conflicts
You coach and encourage us through deliberate practice by . . .	Making an illustrated timeline of the Revolutionary era
	Making a cardboard jigsaw-puzzle map of the colonies and the American continent
	Reading or viewing historical fiction or biography set in that era
	Creating a political advertisement for the views of a major figure in the Revolution
You give us an audience and check our mastery by . . .	Having small groups draw from memory a map of the American continent, illustrating what happened where and when
	Having a debate in which key players in the Revolution take sides on important issues

Practicing Toward Mastery

A worksheet for teachers with students

You want us to know . . .	
You draw us in by . . .	
You help us set reachable goals by . . .	
You ask us to practice the knowledge and skills by . . .	
You check our mastery of important knowledge and skills by . . .	
You chart our small successes by . . .	

◆ NOTE: *To download this worksheet as a pdf, please go to www.firesinthemind.org*

As we came to the end of our conversations about practice in the classroom, however, students realized that one major question remained on the table: Did homework too qualify as deliberate practice? Because it generally took place outside of class—and because it raised strong feelings among students, teachers, and families—we agreed to treat homework separately, in the chapter that follows.

Our Goals for Practice in Class

A checklist by students for teachers

Do we see the meaning and value in the material you introduce?

- ☐ You begin with a story, conflict, or puzzle that goes to the heart of it.
- ☐ You ask for ideas about how it might connect to our lives and interests.
- ☐ You introduce us to people whose work involves this knowledge or skill.
- ☐ You suggest class projects that would help us explore the material.
- ☐ You encourage us to adapt your project ideas, or propose our own.

Do we know what excellent work with this material looks like?

- ☐ You show us the work of real-world masters who use these ideas or skills.
- ☐ You share with us exemplary work by other students.
- ☐ You ask us for good examples we have seen outside of school.
- ☐ You write with us a clear rubric describing the qualities of good work.

Do we know what to practice so we can put our learning to use?

- ☐ You give us each a clear goal that we can expect to succeed at.
- ☐ You give us the chance to explore the material in different ways.
- ☐ You get us to tell you what we don't yet know.
- ☐ You break down what we have to learn into manageable parts or stages.

Do you know what we understand and don't understand?

- ☐ You listen while we explain things to each other.
- ☐ You have us write directions for how to do some part of the work.
- ☐ You arrange Socratic seminars, debates, and other ways to discuss the work.
- ☐ You use homework and pop quizzes for diagnosis but not for grades.

Do you coach us in what we don't yet understand?

- ☐ You have us play games that involve using the concepts and skills.
- ☐ You let us explore and discover in groups, through experiments and research.
- ☐ You have us demonstrate successful techniques to our peers.
- ☐ Your worksheets are short and give us only one thing to practice.
- ☐ You pair us up to practice skills together.
- ☐ You work with us one-on-one when we need it.
- ☐ You give us time in class for reading, writing, research, and problem solving.

Do you ask us to assess our progress and that of our peers?

- ☐ You have us assess ourselves on the basis of the rubric we developed together.
- ☐ You ask us to reflect on what new things we have learned.
- ☐ You ask us to describe where we need to practice more.
- ☐ You ask us to suggest what kind of help you need.
- ☐ You ask us for feedback on how to teach the material better.

◆ NOTE: *To download this checklist as a pdf, please go to www.firesinthemind.org*

CHAPTER EIGHT

Is Homework Deliberate Practice?

F ROM OUR EARLIER WORK together my student collaborators knew that getting good at something takes long hours of deliberate practice. To solidify their skills in the outside activities they pursued, they often worked for hours on their own time. Jacob, for example, played in a neighborhood basketball league in New York City.

> **WHAT KIDS TELL US**
>
> **It's always been a predetermined assignment: "This is what you're going to do." It's always on the whiteboard even before you get into class, and it's not necessarily what students need at that point.**
>
> — BRIDGET

> When I finish a game, I make notes on what I did bad. I ask my friends what I need help in. Then, when I'm alone, I practice by myself. If I'm bad at free throws, I take fifty free throws. If I'm bad at three-pointers, I take a lot of three-pointers. My stamina is not that good, so I push myself by running in the park every day.
> — JACOB

Ideally, kids agreed, their homework for school classes should serve the same function: pushing them to reach a new place that was just within their capability. But when we applied the criteria for deliberate practice to their typical assignments, the homework typically fell far short. The students summarized the situation on the following page.

Is Our Homework Really Practice?

Deliberate practice looks like this ...	but homework often looks like this
It has an express purpose.	We don't know the point of doing it.
It's geared to the individual.	Everyone gets the same homework tasks, no matter what each person needs to work on.
It involves attention and focus.	We can do it without thinking.
It requires repetition or rehearsal.	We're repeating something just to get it over with, not to perfect and remember it.
It requires careful timing.	It takes more time than we have to do it.
It leads to new skills.	We don't use it for anything after it's done.

What would it take to turn homework into the kind of practice that would help students strengthen their skills and knowledge in academic subjects? Perhaps the most powerful steps in that direction would occur, we speculated, when students could start to think of homework as "getting good" at something—and when teachers could welcome feedback from kids on what best supports that developing mastery. In the following sections, students join that conversation with many perspectives from their own experiences.

WHAT'S THE HOMEWORK FOR?

My student collaborators often did not know the point of the homework their teachers assigned them. To feel motivated to do it, they said, they had to believe that the work mattered.

> We need homework that is important, that helps us toward a certain goal we have to meet. The homework that's given can seem random, like a non sequitur—it has nothing to do with anything.
> — CLAUDE

They especially resented homework assignments that seemed like busywork.

> I think a lot of these drills are intended to keep kids focused on something, and to keep them out of trouble: "Let's just give them something to do." — BRIDGET

Kristian objected when her sign language teacher made students copy out material from a book on sign language etiquette.

> The repetition in this case wasn't helping me use sign language better. If you really want me to learn it, ask me to practice it with someone in real life—maybe go to an event where they use sign language. — KRISTIAN

Above all, students believed that homework should match whatever they individually needed to work on. Instead, they said, teachers usually handed out the same homework to everyone.

> I don't think I've ever had a teacher who's geared the homework specifically for what I'm missing. It's always been a predetermined assignment: "This is what you're going to do." It's always on the whiteboard even before you get into class, and it's not necessarily what students need at that point. — BRIDGET

> I need help with atomic radius in chemistry, and another girl has a problem with some other topic. But the teacher doesn't know our weaknesses and what we're good at. The homework, it's just a general "what we need to know." We all learn at different paces, and in different ways, so centralize on what *we* need to learn and how the homework is going to help *us*. — VIVIAN

These students did recognize that practicing certain things outside of school would move them ahead. When they saw that homework helped them, they felt the same motivation to do it that they experienced in other learning activities, such as dance or sports. Christina, for example, treated homework with a perfunctory attitude if she didn't feel she needed that practice. But she actually took it more seriously if she was having trouble in a subject.

> If I already get something perfectly, I'll just do the homework on the bus on the way to school. But if I don't understand something in class, or if I'm just getting to understand it, I'll do my homework, hand it in, and if I get it wrong I'll try again.
> — CHRISTINA

Because students need practice in different aspects of the work, Kristian said, homework tasks should reflect that variety.

> Ideally the teacher would know individual students enough to say, "Let me give you this worksheet, because it will help you." If you were to leave it up to us to pick the one we have the most trouble with, I don't think we'll pick the one that we need. — KRISTIAN

Small groups might work together on assignments, focusing on what each student needed most, Aaron suggested.

> Small groups of peers could help each other do the assignment. It could either be the people that are bad at one thing all grouped together, or people from varying levels in one group, like if I'm good at pronunciation and someone else was really good at conjugating. — AARON R.

One assignment could also address the different needs of many students if it allowed learning in a variety of ways, Claude noted. For example, his English class was working on a multipart project in which the homework took different forms.

You can choose an essay or you can do a poem. And for one part
you do an artistic representation of what you wrote. With more
options and more choices, it might open up learning, and wanting to do things, to *all* students, not just a certain specific group.
— CLAUDE

NO FOLLOW-UP, NO GAIN

When a teacher did not follow up on their homework, students felt
they were left hanging. Did it matter whether they had done it? Why?

> The next day some teachers barely look at it. You worked so hard
> to get it done and they just look and say, "Oh, you did it, fine." It's
> like it's just for nothing. — VIVIAN

Naturally students wanted teacher feedback on the homework they
turned in.

> So many of us have no idea what's going on! And when we don't go
> over homework in class, it feels like we're being ignored. — KRISTIAN

> She has to keep moving forward, she has to stay on her path. But
> there are some of us that fell through the cracks, and we're like,
> "Wait, come back, rewind, so I can get what I need!" — CLAUDE

Without an explicit teacher response, Kristian said, her homework
did not seem like deliberate practice.

> I really want the teacher to evaluate it so I can know what I'm
> doing wrong. From there she can go over what we need, and
> maybe create another homework assignment to explore some-
> thing that we didn't get. — KRISTIAN

And unless a teacher intervened, said Christina, practicing something wrong in a homework assignment could be worse than not
practicing it at all.

> Until you understand what you're doing wrong and how you can change it, you're just going to continually do it wrong and think that you're doing it right. — CHRISTINA

Following up on homework, however, could not realistically entail one-on-one feedback from teacher to students on each assignment. Instead, students said, the classroom should resemble an orchestra rehearsal, with the conductor and those who are practicing working together to identify what needs improvement and make it happen. Teacher and students would then *share* the responsibility of using homework to diagnose problems of understanding. And teachers should act on that information right away.

Students felt much more willing to work on homework when their teachers consistently went over it and helped them learn from it. Working out the problems people had, Nick said, helped to solidify the knowledge he needed to move forward.

> We investigate the problems we did as a class and try to figure out how to get through them. You know why you got the problems wrong. You know what to do about it next time. The concepts will always pop up again later. You learn projectile motion and then start learning things that build up on top of it, so you have to get projectile motion down. — NICK

WHEN HOMEWORK ISN'T FAIR

Evaluating their homework for diagnostic purposes made a lot of sense, these teenagers agreed. But grading their homework defeated its learning purpose. From their activities outside of school they knew that making mistakes played an important part in learning to do something well. Still, it wasn't fair to make them worry about getting a low grade on a task they were just learning.

> It feels like teachers are contradicting themselves when they take off points because you get a homework answer wrong. They're saying, "Stay up, do my homework, and then come back with it all right." That's not practice, that's more like a test that comes at the wrong time! — NICHOLAS

If teachers have to give homework, they should support the risks that kids take in doing it, said Erika.

> My teacher would give us a worksheet for homework, but he didn't count answers wrong. He gave you credit for trying, which I think helped me. I was more willing to try because I knew that if I got it wrong, he was going to take time to make sure that I understood it. He offered a lot of help in tutoring and stuff. — ERIKA

Grading homework had an even worse effect, kids said. It fostered dishonest or cynical behavior on the part of both teachers and students.

> Some homework is just busywork, to give us more grades. The end of the quarter comes and teachers say, "I don't really have enough grades to put in, so now I need you guys to do this worksheet, this, this, this, and this." — AARON R.

> It took me five hours to do this really difficult math homework and I still didn't understand it, but I was trying my best. Another girl totally copied it off the Internet—she got 100 and I got a 39. If I ask her, she doesn't understand it. But the teacher doesn't care how many hours we spent on it—she's looking at if you got it right or wrong. So, in the long haul, who's smarter—me or the chick who copied it off the computer? — VIVIAN

For students who couldn't get the homework done because of their family circumstances, a bad grade on homework felt like one more card in a deck stacked against them. Dina's parents both worked sixteen-hour days as home health aides, and she spent her evenings making the family dinner, doing laundry, and supervising younger children.

> I do my homework on the bus, but that's not enough time—and usually I fall asleep before it's done. That's why my grades aren't so good, even though I want to go to college. – DINA

Many thought that the requirement to take work home was also unfair to students who had no one to help them with their questions. Family members often cannot provide the help that students need when they are working at academic tasks, said Rachel.

> When you're home it's harder to ask questions if you're having trouble. I can't ask my parents; they don't know about math, they don't know what I'm reading in school. I can call a friend. But it's not the same as being in the actual learning environment with everyone else around you. – RACHEL M.

Students also said they got more out of their academic practice when they could do it in collaboration with others.

> Group homework doesn't pile it all on one person, it divides the work up evenly. You have different ideas, you get to communicate, and you feed off each other. – CLAUDE

> Students helping other students, you connect with them, because you *know* them, you can understand their problems, so you could break it down the way they understand it. You get your work done twice as fast, it's much easier, and you all share your knowledge.
> – JACOB

But arranging a time and space for group homework often proved nearly impossible for students with different commitments and far-flung home locations.

Given all of these considerations, many students believed that doing additional academic work at home was penalizing them for things beyond their control. Because kids did realize the value of extra practice, however, we tried to come up with better ways for them to get the practice they needed outside of class. (See sidebar, page 126.)

SO MUCH HOMEWORK, SO LITTLE TIME

In addition to their concerns about equity, other factors made taking work home both unrealistic and counterproductive, my students said. They recognized that effective practice was not necessarily enjoyable, but they didn't think they learned much when exhausted.

> I don't want to continue my school day at home! I burn out as soon as I get home at four o'clock. I understand the benefits of having homework—the deliberate practice, improving yourself, and increasing your knowledge. But definitely I'm not going to spend more than two hours a night on school. – RACHEL M.

> I get home and I'm knocked out. I don't even *want* to do my homework, and my body doesn't want to do it either. – CLAUDE

Faced with an overload, students such as Vivian made nightly choices about which homework to rush through, or put aside completely.

> I get home from soccer practice at seven o'clock and I really don't feel like doing all that homework. I'm like, "Okay, what's more important, math or history?" My eyes are closing but I just push myself to stay up late. Sometimes I drink coffee, so it's unhealthy too! – VIVIAN

When she did try to bulldoze through an assignment, said Vivian, she often found she didn't get much out of it.

Doing Our Homework at School

Many students thought that, rather than sending students home with assignments, it would be more fair for teachers to provide times and places at school for their academic practice and preparation. They came up with these suggestions:

- ☐ **Give us time in class to practice.** After the main part of a lesson, allow twenty minutes for kids to practice the knowledge or skills involved. Let us work in groups or by ourselves, depending on our needs. Watch where we are having trouble and take steps to help.

- ☐ **Schedule a regular period into every school day for academic support.** We could select (or be assigned) this elective to give us a quiet space with access to teachers and peer tutors. Don't label it as remedial, just as time for independent study. Provide breakout spaces for students who are working in groups.

- ☐ **Schedule an extended period once weekly for students to have access to teachers and peer tutors.** This is like the daily academic support period, but it takes place once a week for a longer time.

- ☐ **Provide an after-school support program.** We could choose to do our homework here, or teachers could assign it if we are falling behind. Teachers and peer tutors should be present to help if we need it. Again, students working in groups will need breakout spaces.

When I'm doing math homework, I go fast and crazy, and in the end I still don't understand it, really. It's just a lot of pressure. And it shows: I'm always tired in class because I spent all my night doing my homework! Teachers don't see "Vivian totally understands that." They see "Vivian *did* her homework."

— VIVIAN

Joe was more willing to do his math homework, he said, because his teacher parceled it out over time, in manageable pieces.

I don't think that people can handle massive amounts of correction at one time. You're going to have to feed it to us by the spoon. My teacher just gives me a couple of things that I should work on: "You need a little bit of help on this and I will walk you through it." I work on those things, I get better at them, then she gives me a couple more. — JOE

"It's better to understand what you're doing than to get the homework done," agreed Claude. Teachers and students could have it both ways, he proposed: less homework but geared toward deeper understanding.

One focused question can make you think as much as twenty or thirty homework questions combined! And it shows more understanding, instead of just having questions where you can just copy other people's understanding. Then everybody can contribute to the question in class—you look at what other people say and it adds to your understanding. — CLAUDE

THE FOUR R'S OF HOMEWORK AS PRACTICE

At its best, students agreed, their additional work after a lesson could be like practicing a sport or a musical instrument. It shouldn't ask them to try something they weren't ready for. (They knew that if they started out doing it wrong, it would take a very long time to undo.) Instead, it should add value to their lessons through what we decided to call the "four R's" of deliberate practice:

- *Readying* themselves for new learning
- *Repetition* and application of knowledge and skills
- *Reviewing* material learned earlier
- *Revising* their work

We agreed that if homework always fit into one of those categories, it would yield the best results. Students' practice would always be aimed at acquiring new knowledge, applying new skills, and creating their best work with what they knew and could do.

Readying students for new learning. Students understood that teachers wanted them to be ready to participate in class. Doing her chemistry homework ahead of time, Vivian said, helped her come to class better equipped to learn.

> The homework takes me really long, because I'm constantly reading and looking at my notes and stuff. But I have to admit that when I'm in class, I understand everything better. It's in my head already because I studied it so much last night. And most of her test questions come from the homework, so in the long haul it really helps me. – VIVIAN

Jacob's English teacher asked students to read a poem carefully in preparation for a class discussion.

> When we first read it, many people didn't even know what the poem was about. It was so complicated. But we practiced breaking it down, stanza by stanza, and then in class it all came together. We looked deep into the meaning of each stanza, and that way people start understanding it. – JACOB

Repetition. Just repeating something again and again did not make it come back to them automatically, students said. They also had to be paying attention to what they were repeating, and how. Like hitting a tennis ball again and again over the net, their most effective homework asked students to practice new skills and knowledge as problems came at them in different ways.

> My economics teacher gave us three or four worksheets a night. It was a bit much, but I know the stuff really well now. I did the

graphs so many times, I know them backwards and forwards. I
think with those kind of subjects, economics and math, you need
the repetition to really understand it, to be able to do it any which
way it's given to you. — BRIDGET

Students often had the hardest time engaging when teachers
asked them to learn information by heart. The memorization task
got somewhat better, they said, if they could manage to connect the
material to something that had meaning to them. When Christian
had to learn to identify paintings for an art history test, for example,
he imagined the paintbrush in his own hand.

I try to place myself in the period, like, "What's the typical thing I
would see in the Renaissance time?" I'll see the lineup of the fig-
ures, the little things that a person would know in that period. I
start thinking of paintings I could have done—I have my own
opinions, like, "This should've been here, this should've been
there." — CHRISTIAN

Often, however, students could not come up with a meaningful connection to even those things they recognized as important:
verb tenses, or the elements of the periodic table, or important
names and dates.

In your mind it's kind of harder to remember, because you're not
actually seeing it and you're not actually doing it. — DYLAN

In cases like this, Bridget said, it helped to have the class and the
teacher come up with a bag of memory tricks from which individual
students could choose.

I think you know what works and what doesn't for you. You have
proven strategies that you can apply to learning any material.
Maybe you know that making flash cards works for you, so you
use that for anything. — BRIDGET

Review. Even while learning new skills, students realized, they also needed to keep practicing the ones they had learned before. Christina compared some homework to her warm-ups in dance.

> Every day we do the same things at the barre that we've been doing since we were little. Even when you're getting better as a dancer, you still have to keep up that practice. Otherwise it's easy to get lazy about little things, and you can mess up how the dance looks.
> — CHRISTINA

For Claude, reviewing the basics of algebra outside of class helped him keep up as the class moved into new territory.

> At an early age, I had a difficult time and I didn't get those basic math skills that most kids have. So now I struggle with certain things, like algebraic equations. I have to constantly go over them at home to remember the steps on how to do them. — CLAUDE

Revision. From the out-of-school activities they cared about, students already had experience with revising their work. If something wasn't coming out right in knitting or in a building project, they were used to going back and trying again. When her teacher made the class revise an essay, Christina said, she thought of it as the same thing.

> When I write I tend to just throw in every single little detail that I possibly can. All my essays have so many run-on sentences, and sentences that don't even make sense! So I go back, like, "Well, this doesn't make any sense so I'm not going to put this in there," or "Maybe I can change this up so it's more relevant to what I'm supposed to be writing about." — CHRISTINA

HOMEWORK WE ACTUALLY WANT TO DO

Occasionally, my students said, something they did in school inspired and energized them to the point that they wanted to go home and keep working on it. "If it's really strong and exciting and hands-on stuff, then I'll do it!" said Nicholas, reflecting on his chemistry class.

> When she's talking about atoms and ions, she writes words! We copy from an overhead projector into a notebook, and then she says that it's all trends and stuff like that. I'm like, "This is so boring." I need to see the trend, I need to really understand what *is* an atom, an ion. If I don't, then nothing's going to work out in my head! But some of the demos that we do, I love that. I can actually see what's going on, and that's the kind of homework that works for me. – NICHOLAS

Christina and Nicholas both remembered a global studies unit on the French Revolution in which students acted out a courtroom trial of the king and queen. The project brought even routine homework assignments to life, they said.

> I was the queen. So of course I wanted to do my homework all the time, so I could know the facts of what happened and what didn't happen, know what I wanted to say when someone tried to say I did this or that thing. I could say, "Oh no, I didn't!"—because I'd read my homework. – CHRISTINA

> It required a lot of question answering and I loved to do it because it was so interesting. He gave us different packets of questions and you had to go back to find the answers in the passages. When a teacher gives you the answer, you can't go anywhere to find it—you know it already, which makes it a lot less fun. – NICHOLAS

When school curriculum was framed in such active and involving ways, these students began to see that academic subjects too could elicit the same absorbed attention that they gave to their favorite activities outside school. In the next chapter they will tell us

Alternatives to Traditional Homework

The Situation	Instead of This Homework	Try This	When and Where
You introduced new material to us in class.	Assigning a question set so we will remember the material.	Ask *us* to think up a homework task that follows up on this class. What would our task look like? Why are we assigning it?	Model this in class, then have us come up with ideas. Use our best ideas as subsequent assignments.
You want us to read an article before a class discussion.	Making us answer questions that prove we have read it.	Ask us to write down two or three questions *we* have after reading it.	We can text or e-mail you the questions before discussing the article in class.
You want to see if we understand a key concept (such as literary irony, checks and balances in government, the turn of seasons, mathematical functions).	Making us complete a worksheet.	Ask us to demonstrate the concept for the class in small groups, using any medium we choose (drama, art, writing, games).	Not a final assessment but a quick activity in class, so we can review the concept together and you can tell if we understand.

◆ NOTE: *To download this worksheet as a pdf, please go to www.firesinthemind.org*

The Situation	Instead of This Homework	Try This	When and Where
You have demonstrated a mathematical procedure and you want us to see how it applies in various situations.	Assigning us ten word problems that involve this procedure.	Ask small groups to choose from your examples *one* word problem where this procedure applies in the real world, then solve it and present it to the class.	In class, so you can coach us as we work through the problem and help clarify any confusions when we present.
You want us to memorize facts (such as dates in history, spelling or grammar, vocabulary, elements of the periodic table).	Handing out a list that we will be tested on later.	Ask each of us to create and share with the class a memorization trick (such as music, acronym, visual cue, gesture; cognate) that works for *us* with at least one item on this list.	In class or outside school, by ourselves or in small groups.
You want us to remember what you taught us last month.	Assigning a review sheet at the end of the unit.	Give us frequent *short* pop quizzes about earlier material. Go over the quiz with us right afterward, but don't count the grade.	In class, so every few days you see and address what we have forgotten.

◆ NOTE: *To download this worksheet as a pdf, please go to www.firesinthemind.org*

more about how projects in particular brought them into that new relationship with their learning and began to turn school into a workplace that fostered the habits of experts that we have been studying throughout this book.

Homework Advice from Students

☐ Make sure we know what purpose the homework serves. Write it at the top of the assignment so we remember it!

☐ Use our homework! Look at it, answer our questions, and show us why it matters.

☐ Don't take off points for wrong answers on homework. It's practice!

☐ Cooperate with other teachers so our total homework load is reasonable.

☐ Give us time to start our homework in class so you can help if we have trouble. When appropriate, assign different tasks to match what each of us needs.

☐ Match homework to the time we have available. Let us know how long you expect us to spend on it, and don't penalize us if we can't finish.

☐ Don't give us homework every day. Having several days to do it helps us learn to manage our time.

☐ Create places in school for sustained academic support: tutoring time, study halls, hours when you are always available for help.

◆ NOTE: *To download this checklist as a pdf, please go to www.firesinthemind.org*

CHAPTER NINE

School Projects That Build Expert Habits

A T THIS POINT IN OUR Practice Project, my student collaborators knew a lot about what it took to get very good at a challenging activity that really mattered to them. Increasingly they were developing a sense that they could grow strong at whatever they chose to do.

In their academic subjects, however, they knew they had a long way to go. "Whatever we're studying, we won't be experts yet in that field," Kenzie said. To build their base of knowledge and to practice important skills across the curriculum would clearly take an extraordinary amount of focused time, effort, and coaching.

> ## WHAT KIDS TELL US
>
> It's not just one person saying, "We should do it this way." It's everybody saying, "We should try this and try that." Everybody is putting in their own little input, and the final thing that you make will be everybody's together.
>
> — RUBEN

Yet despite moments of real connection with individual teachers, few of these students expressed excitement about the work they did at school. The structure of school itself, we suspected, undercut that possibility. Thousands of hours of class time, if fragmented into disconnected subjects presented in short blocks of time, did not give kids the deliberate practice that most deeply engaged them. And the typical homework they got wasn't helping much.

Interdisciplinary projects at school, however, stood out for them as a remarkable exception. Like their most compelling outside activities, such projects often had kids working toward an outcome that mattered to them. Because they valued the project's goal, they willingly went after the knowledge and skills required to reach it. Along the way they put what they were learning into use, and when they ran into trouble they got encouragement and help. That mix of factors worked well, said Tyler.

> You end up asking a lot of questions. And because you have to ask questions, you end up learning a lot. – TYLER

My student collaborators had often felt bored or disaffected at school, but their minds caught fire when they were asked to take on challenging "real world" projects as part of their academic curriculum. In the next sections we take a look at how they got started on these projects, kept at them through whatever difficulties came up, and began to build serious new knowledge and skills.

PROJECTS START WITH VALUE AND MEANING

Just as with their activities outside school, these students first got interested in a school-related project when something about it struck a chord with them. And here again, the value kids placed on it could come from any direction.

For many the draw was often simply that a project looked like fun. Going into the "real world" to do something active with their peers particularly appealed to them. Even if the topic did not immediately grab them, a group excursion to build new knowledge held much more interest than a classroom lecture.

Whether they were in the classroom or outside the school walls, the moment they viewed a topic in a context that gave it meaning, students found themselves wanting to know more about it. For example, Tyler's eleventh grade class learned that endangered species from the African bush were being sold as meat. That drew them into a yearlong interdisciplinary project that aimed to come up with DNA barcodes to identify animal meat in markets around the world.

"What I love about our school is that my outside interests can occasionally overlap," Tyler said.

> Like, how can we take what we're learning about class in DNA and apply it? If you're doing something that's tied into the real world, you learn a lot from the experience. It's going to involve a lot more than science, or a lot more than just math. It's not an assignment—it's like you have ownership over the project. – TYLER

Often the culminating goal of the project—a trip, a performance, a competition—lent a group energy and purpose from the start. For Alex, each new production his drama class took on started a new cycle of motivation and effort.

> Everyone cares, because it's a real thing. We have to get it done, so there's that need to work together. You're not doing it alone. – ALEX

Students have told us again and again throughout this book that just such social factors led them to place high value on working hard to do something well. We devote the rest of this chapter to exploring why team projects prove so compelling as a curricular strategy for adolescent learners.

TEAM PROJECTS AS A SCAFFOLD FOR EXPERT HABITS

From our previous investigations, we knew the habits that experts called on when they set out to solve challenges in the real world. We had seen how mastery developed step by step as people reached for each new task they were ready to take on. With coaching and practice, we now saw, even very different kinds of students were using team projects to help each other rise to excellence in ways like this:

- They started with a question, a problem, or a challenge that required extending the understanding of the group.

- Team members not only had individual parts to play but also traded off tasks as they worked toward a common goal. They cooperated to fill in gaps in their knowledge and build new competence.

- They adapted to changes and made new discoveries as conditions shifted during the course of the project.

- They forged bonds within the group as shared challenge created deeper investment in the work itself.

- They reflected on the process and the outcome of the project after a culminating product, performance, or presentation.

As with an athletic team or a musical ensemble, these students saw their individual strengths as a vital part of the success of the project. The teamwork itself, they realized, helped generate a kind of "group expertise."

> What I may not be able to do, somebody else can. If I need help, I go to them, and if I can do something that other people can't, they are going to come to me. — RUBEN

The more they felt that their contribution mattered, the more motivated they were to do it well.

> If you're in charge of one task, your group depends on you to get that task done. If one person doesn't do their job, the project will fail. — ERIKA

Most interesting was that students who worked on such projects reported a level of absorbed engagement that matched their experiences of flow outside of school. That reward was worth all the effort that the best projects demanded, Tyler said.

> You just stop perceiving time. It doesn't seem to go by fast or slow, even when you're tired. And physical things also become irrelevant. You become so focused that you don't notice anything going on around you. You forget to eat, forget to take breaks. – TYLER

As they describe their work on challenging projects, we can see these teenagers building an explicit identity as people who work together to do important things well. In the following sections they tell how their teachers coached them through the process of becoming an expert team.

TEAMWORK REQUIRES DELIBERATE PRACTICE

To do a good job on these projects, students said, they needed deliberate practice in negotiating the dynamics of a working group. The teamwork challenges are considerable, said Kristian, whose San Antonio high school grounds its curriculum in projects.

> We have to work in groups with people we may not necessarily want to be with. You could have a struggle for leadership, like, "Who's gonna take charge of this project?" You have to look back at other experiences and figure out, "How did I do it in this situation? How did I work with somebody that gets on my nerves?" – KRISTIAN

For this reason, their teachers explicitly coached them in collaboration skills from ninth grade on.

> We weren't really told, "This is what it takes to make a good group," but we were taught a lot of skills, like how to come to consensus. We had a whole lesson about whether or not a group should vote on things. Like, what are the benefits of everyone

debating on what should be done and coming to a consensus, and what are the benefits of one person just taking the lead in what we're going to do? I think that was helpful in learning how to work in a group and negotiate things. — ERIKA

As new ninth graders, Evangelina's New York City class went on a three-day camping retreat so they could focus on working out just those issues. The experience opened her eyes, she said.

You don't have to know everything. You work together, making as much effort as possible to put things together. It was all about getting along, having to communicate. We all had a say in what we could do. It took us a while, and in the end we succeeded, even though some people had wanted to give up. — EVANGELINA

BUILDING KNOWLEDGE AS A TEAM

Like team projects in the world of work, these school-related projects required participants to gather and use knowledge in many different ways. Students were simultaneously using their individual strengths and growing in understanding from the work that others were doing.

Here again their teachers played an important coaching role. For example, when assigning research tasks to build the team's base of knowledge, they took care that students at every level could expect to manage them successfully.

We started with baby steps and worked up, year by year. First it was, "Here's the articles; this is the information you should gather." Then, "Here's where you can find the information," and then, "This is the question I want you to find." Finally, it was, "Have fun, go for what you want to find out." So all throughout the years that's how we've been getting good at researching. — BRIDGET

Many projects entailed going beyond conventional sources of information and gaining access to resources in the community.

We had to contact people and negotiate with them and put things together. That wasn't easy, but we all were expected to learn. – NICK

In a regular classroom routine these students shared their growing knowledge with others on their project team.

We had weekly or so meetings and sometimes we would have what we call "big teaches," when the class all comes together and we divide into our groups. The teacher was just there to facilitate it, to make sure these things were done in a timely fashion. – AARON R.

CREATING NEW WORK TOGETHER

As they combined their knowledge in such ways, students began to realize that they were doing far more than plugging the holes in their information base. They were also generating new knowledge and making new sense of what they learned. And in that process they were finding new intellectual satisfactions in the company of their peers.

To have an interdependent group of people that are maybe not experts but competent in certain areas, it definitely makes a difference in how certain ideas or a solution might come out. – AARON R.

When we make a project together, it's not just one person saying, "We should do it this way." It's everybody saying, "We should try this and try that." Everybody is putting in their own little input, and the final thing that you make will be everybody's together. – RUBEN

The excitement of exploring new territory together, students said, helped them keep up the work even when it grew difficult and intense. Molly spoke about her state of flow in the last stages of a robotics project she worked on.

You really don't notice when you're here for two days straight, because you're working on finishing. It becomes something that

How Does Our Knowledge Grow?

Students analyze how expert knowledge develops

Formal Knowledge

- ☐ We gain information from texts or lectures.
- ☐ Information comes alive when we put it into practice.
- ☐ We use information to gain access to more information.

Informal Knowledge

- ☐ We know things from common sense.
- ☐ We pick up skills or information by doing things.
- ☐ We gain knowledge from watching others and asking questions.
- ☐ We may not formulate what we know and can do, so it can be hard to teach.

Impressions

- ☐ We tune in to what's around us.
- ☐ We notice patterns and draw conclusions from them.
- ☐ We follow our hunches about what might work out.

Group Knowledge

- ☐ We combine our knowledge with that of others in our group.
- ☐ We generate new knowledge as a group.

Self-Knowledge

- ☐ We plan how to work on the knowledge and skills we lack.
- ☐ We practice the habit of thinking things through.
- ☐ We try out our thoughts with others.
- ☐ We notice patterns in how we learn.

◆ NOTE: *To download this checklist as a pdf, please go to www.firesinthemind.org*

you're so proud of. Finally, after you have left whatever project you have been working on, you go home and you're still thinking about it. That's the last thing you think about before you sleep. – MOLLY

THE ROLE OF PERFORMANCE IN STUDENT PROJECTS

These student teams also cared about how the end products of their projects would be received. From our investigation of performance, discussed in Chapter Six, they had gained a strong sense of its role in the process of developing expertise. Showing what they knew and could do—whether in front of an audience or through some other real-world application or product—was a natural extension of the many hours of practice they had put into their learning projects.

Those for whom projects were a regular part of their work at school noticed their public presentation skills steadily growing. It was not talent but practice that brought them to that point, said Moira.

> Plenty of people in our school are uncomfortable with public speaking. But it's required, so you have to overcome that if you want to succeed. And it's worked. Even though there are kids in our class that you might not consider excellent public speakers, they're way better than they were when we started four years ago.
> – MOIRA

However, applause for a public presentation was not enough. It seemed mere blanket praise, without distinction among the different elements of a project. After all they had put into their projects, they hoped for a mix of coaching and critique, appreciation and evaluation.

Would they get credit for the skills they had practiced throughout: their teamwork, their independent research, their organization and creation of a product, and its presentation? Who would give them feedback on the content knowledge they had gained along the

Criteria for a First-Rate Project

- ☐ We clearly state the central question that our project addresses.

- ☐ We collaborate on planning and carrying out the project.

- ☐ We gather evidence from several primary and secondary sources, including at least one interview with an expert in the field.

- ☐ We set deadlines for all project tasks and meet them.

- ☐ We seek out critique along the way and revise our work as needed.

- ☐ We deliver a product or performance that thoroughly addresses the project's central question.

- ☐ We give evidence that our project had a positive impact.

- ☐ We reflect on our process and our product.

way in various fields? Would anyone suggest a direction in which they might take their learning next?

Drawing on rubrics from many different student projects, we came up with our own criteria to describe excellence across an array of possible projects. (See above.)

SAMPLE PROJECTS TO INSPIRE PRACTICE

Of the many students who worked on our Practice Project, only about 20 percent had worked on a challenging project as part of their school curriculum. But for those who did, the experience stayed with them. When we analyzed the expert process in other settings—by looking at their outside-school activities or by listening to expert adults describe their work—these students often drew comparisons to their school projects. And as they told of the projects, they could also make connections with the work outside of school.

Below we describe a number of group projects that stood out, along with several individual projects completed by students.

The Traffic Project

Could students from a high school economics class help resolve San Antonio's growing traffic problem? "We already have a lot of informal knowledge about traffic, just from getting to school every day," said Nick, a member of the class that took up that question in the Traffic Project, a study in microeconomic decision making that began with the students' own experience and ended with their formal presentations to the board of the city's transportation authority.* "We've driven around, we know what traffic is like."

To build on their informal knowledge, however, students needed to find out more about the history and politics of their city's inefficient system of roads. Their teacher arranged a series of visiting speakers to provide a base of information.

> Even though our economics teacher might not be an expert about traffic, he brought in four or five experts from the City Council and the Transportation people for us to talk to. That was a good thing to do before we started our independent research. — RACHEL M.

Then, in teams of three or four, students asked their own questions, gathered their own evidence, and worked through their own ideas about the transportation decisions they and their city were making.

> We had a set of questions and we started off with our own ideas, trying to find an alternative way to help with the traffic problem. We came together and bounced them off each other, and that really helped the project come together. — KAREN

---

*The Traffic Project was designed and taught in spring 2009 by Will Maddox, a graduate student in education at Trinity University who was student teaching at the International School of the Americas in San Antonio, Texas.

I ride my bike mainly as my transportation, so for my group I talked about that, that was my form of expertise, that's how I would gather evidence on how our roads are not really equipped for bicyclists. And two people in my group drive to school. So that's how they would gather evidence on the congestion problem.
— AARON R.

At the same time, their teacher was introducing in class the economic concepts of scarcity, efficiency, supply and demand, and opportunity cost that the traffic problem illustrated. As student teams tried out their thoughts on reducing road travel, they increasingly applied these new terms to evaluate potential solutions. What resources would their proposals require? Would government manage it, or a private company? What incentives would promote its use, and who would pay its costs?

We had to break down the costs, like what fuels may be used, and then think about what we would have to do to make what we proposed happen. — KAREN

To prime the pump for ideas and enrich their background knowledge, students read portions of Tim Harford's accessible book *The Undercover Economist*. Occasionally the teacher would also suggest possibilities for teams to consider.

He would pose an out-of-the-box solution, asking, "What happens if. . . ?" What if you taxed every driver on how many miles they drove? We thought that was a good idea. I also thought that refurbishing the buses in San Antonio was a good idea. Right now they kind of look worn down and I think that's one reason why people don't ride them. — NICK

Each team crafted a six-page written proposal to city officials, with the option of using a different medium as long as it met the objectives for the project. They tried hard, they said, to live up to the criteria their teacher presented on his assessment rubrics: understanding of economic principles, strong critical analysis, maximum feasibility of the proposal, persuasive writing, and a collaborative group presentation that showed excellent oral communication.

Presenting to the transportation board raised the stakes even higher, Kristian said.

> First I have to translate this technical mumbo-jumbo into something I can understand. And then we have to translate what I understand, or what my group understands, into something formal so that we don't look stupid when we go and talk to City Council. — KRISTIAN

As part of the project's final assessment, students also evaluated one another's contributions to their learning team.

> Afterward they gave us sheets where we were expected to evaluate, rather thoroughly, the people who worked with us in our groups. They taught us how to grade people—and grade ourselves too—on how well we aid the group. — NICK

The evaluation rubric assessed more than participation and collaboration, however. Students also explicitly noted how well team members used individual strengths in carrying out the project's work while improving in their weaker areas as well. As the project ended its six-week span, these teenagers had given a robust example of the energy and new learning generated in an academic content area by practicing together as an "expert team."

A Field Guide to the Bay

Holding a meter-square contraption made of white PVC pipes, a few students crouched over a patch of tide-washed sand, counting the limpets and barnacles they found within the transect. Up the shore, classmates were using a laser leveling device and a pole to measure off the tide's height at regular intervals. Other kids poked around the water's edge, turning over rocks or following the path of a shorebird. Several solitary students sat at a distance with notebooks, writing or drawing in response to the urban seascape before them.

For an entire spring semester, the eleventh grade teaching team at a high school in urban San Diego centered its math, science, and humanities coursework on this ambitious investigative project in which students would create and publish a field guide to the nearby San Diego Bay.*

Filled with color photographs, maps, and charts, the guide stood on its own as a naturalist's guide, identifying, analyzing, and quantifying the life forms found in the bay's intertidal zones and harbors. A student-written history of mapmaking by early explorers segued into an overview of present-day biogeography, with students using sophisticated mapmaking technology to represent their data. And in the tradition of the adventurer's log, students offered their own perspectives on the worlds they observed, in reflections, poems, and political commentary.

The project began with students examining strong models from across the disciplines. In the previous year, the humanities class read *The Log from the Sea of Cortez*, a 1940 travel log written by John Steinbeck and his friend Ed Ricketts, director of Pacific Biological Laboratories. The following year, students pored over Jared Diamond's *Collapse*, applying its benchmarks for the decline of societies to the situation of the San Diego Bay.

---

*The Field Guide to the San Diego Bay project took place in the spring 2005 semester at High Tech High in San Diego. It was designed and led by three eleventh grade teachers: biology teacher Jay Vavra, humanities teacher Tom Fehrenbacher, and math teacher Rod Buenviaje.

In biology class, students read and critiqued some twenty other guides for naturalists. Several calculus students used Fourier analysis to schedule school-day research trips so they would coincide with the necessary low-low tides. At two local colleges, professors received a National Science Foundation grant to teach the high school researchers how to use Geographic Information System technology.

The young authors also had an explicit public purpose. Given the precarious balance between their city's natural life, industry, and commerce, they wanted to awaken local residents to the potential destruction of their Bay. Josefina noted:

> Most San Diegans have been down to the Bay, but we know very little about its biodiversity or its habitats. — JOSEFINA

Whether observing sponges or pelicans, sea lions or the homeless human population that frequented the Bay, the student participants also cast a thoughtful eye on interdependence and sustainability in San Diego's mix of the military, industry, tourism, and nature. One section described the effects of boat paints on marine life; another took note of how Coronado Island's socioeconomic elite isolates itself from the city's pressing problems.

Even the students' poetic contributions evoked interconnectedness. From the Boat Channel, Khoa wrote:

> I cast my feet and hands into the sea
> Let my head lie by the dry sand
> Wither away wither away
> I have barely made a scratch
> "Will I be remembered?" echoes in the far distant
> From where my reality came. . . .
> — KHOA

At semester's end, the students designed and laid out *Perspectives of the San Diego Bay* using desktop publishing technology and printed the book with the help of a modest grant. With students as its marketers, it found an audience in local stores and won the notice of national environmental groups.

For its authors that meant more than any A on their report cards. "Every kid has that question, 'Where am I going to use this in the real world?'" said Evan, one of the guide's chief student editors.

> Well, you can't get much more attached to the real world than this. My friends are like, "I'm studying for finals," and I'm like, "Well, I'm going to make and publish and print and sell a book!" – EVAN

A Learning Expedition to Washington

Many schools sponsor a class trip to the national's capital, but my student collaborators in San Antonio took that expedition to new levels. Their senior trip to Washington, DC involved them in an extended class project, in which they actively explored the complexities of global citizenship, the overarching theme of their school.*

Small "travel groups" of students researched one of ten guiding questions before and during the trip, choosing from topics that included the millennium development goals of the United Nations: economic development, climate change, water, infectious disease, terrorism, population growth, poverty, education, biological diversity, and illicit markets.

The project built skills in both collaboration and research, students said, as well as stretching their thinking about the challenges and responsibilities of Americans in the larger world. In Washington, each group interviewed officials at two embassies, as well as leaders at a nongovernmental organization in their area of interest.

---

*Curriculum and assessment materials on the Senior Expedition to Washington, D.C., are available from the International School of the Americas (www.neisd.net/isa/index.html).

My question was, "What is the role of developed nations to assist developing nations economically?" We went to two different embassies, Kenya and Denmark, and we talked about how their countries assisted or depended on each other financially. – DEEPIKA

Our group went to the embassy of Haiti, a developing country that [at that time] had increasing population growth, and then to the one for Denmark, a developed country with a decreasing population growth. Then we went to an NGO called Population Connection, that focuses mainly on teaching teachers about population growth. – KRISTIAN

Even their visits to traditional sights, students said, centered on building understanding about how the capital city and its governmental structures and practices function as part of an international network.

Before the trip, teams had shared the information they gathered in weekly "big teaches" in the classroom. After returning home, they formally presented their work at a symposium held at a nearby university.

We had to make twenty-minute presentations and present them to the class, and the teachers had a rubric. Things like, Did we basically explain the whole problem? Did we cover its historical aspects? Did we propose solutions? Did we show what we learned? Did every group member get to speak, and was it well-spoken, was it a good presentation? – BRIDGET

A final element of the project required students, on their return, to take local action on what they had learned about their topic. Aaron's group for biodiversity planted trees around the city, he said, and Bridget's education group created an interactive web site about its findings.

The community can come look at what our group's done, and there's places for people to add to the pages, to comment and start discussions. – BRIDGET

Their trip was a lot of fun, these teenagers agreed. Reflecting on it afterward, some wished for more structured time beforehand to better carry out their role as active researchers in Washington. But they also noted that throughout their high school years other projects had coached them to act like members of an "expert team" on increasingly ambitious projects. Bridget explained:

> Freshman year, all the research was given to us by the teachers, and we were taught how to put it into a project and give a presentation to a panel. As time went on, we had to do the research more on our own. Sophomore year we were given a topic and tools: "Okay, you want to look at these kinds of research tools, look at these sites, this is how to cite your sources." And then junior year we had to make a documentary about the Alabama Civil Rights Project. The teacher gave us a question and said, "Go, make a movie." It was our job to get interviews and gather historical evidence. – BRIDGET

By senior year, the adults who coached this rich academic exploration of the nation's capital were "basically hands-off," Bridget concluded. Her class had truly grown into an expert team: "We were ready to be off on our own."

CHAPTER TEN

Making School a Community of Practice

M Y STUDENT COLLABORATORS had now come full circle in our Practice Project. They had looked closely at the out-of-school activities that most satisfied their own drive to do things well. With a new perspective—and a new vocabulary to describe "getting really good at something"—they had analyzed the habits of adults who rose to excellence in their fields.

> ❝ WHAT KIDS TELL US
>
> **If no one's going to notice what you're doing, it doesn't matter whether you push yourself. But if the teacher develops a connection with you, you don't want to disappoint them.**
>
> — SAMANTHA

Finally, they had scrutinized their own work at school, taking careful note of where it resembled (and did not resemble) the challenges to which they readily rose in other settings.

How should schools change, I asked these teenagers, if their purpose was to inspire students to practice hard and well at things that mattered?

My students' recommendations, with which we close this book, came both from their lived experience and from the understanding they had gained during our investigation. Some are suggestions that individual teachers might carry out in the classroom; others would require an entire learning community to turn in a new direction. These students do not intend to set forth a comprehensive picture of "school reform," however. Instead, they hope to bring a fresh sense of awareness, engagement, and energy into teaching and learning, no matter what their setting. In each piece of advice that follows, we can see their eagerness to enter into a shared community of practice in which young people and adults aim for the same high standards and support each other in the journey toward mastery.

Link school to a purpose that has meaning to us.

> Kids are going to go to school if it's interesting to them. — CHELSEA

> Everyone is just kind of thrown into school and kids don't understand why. That's why they're not really interested; it skews our inner view of what we're looking at. Instead of being forced upon us, school has to be a place where kids would *choose* to go. — MIKE

> In an ideal school, the students know what the purpose is of being in school that day, every day. Once you have that, each classroom can center on that purpose. The administration can recognize the diversity between the students and give them options in what they take. Then, in the classroom, the deliberate practice comes in. You need to teach all kids how to learn, because even one student can make the difference. — RACHEL M.

Keep the community of learners small enough to know each other.

> In order to push ourselves and want to keep trying more difficult things, the teacher needs to make a good connection with the student. If no one's going to notice what you're doing, it doesn't matter whether you push yourself. But if the teacher develops a connection with you, you don't want to disappoint them.
> — SAMANTHA

Make exploring new fields a big part of our learning.

> One way to find your passion is to explore as many things as you can until you find something that you love. By introducing us to stuff that we normally wouldn't know about, you're exposing us to things that we didn't know we might have an interest in. If it wasn't for my economics class, I might never have discovered that this is something that I have a passion for! – BRIDGET

Don't try to cover everything.

> We need enough time to get to a higher level of thinking on a subject. Maybe you won't cover everything, but you'll create an avenue for students to develop their own ideas, without thinking of the teacher as the only source. Teach us how to find information when we need it, so we can access it without having to simply memorize things. – SANA

> Take the kind of things that we learn in our core classes—writing, reading, math, and skills like that—and put them at the base of elective courses instead. Then someone could choose a poetry class, or geology, instead of the more general classes. – KENZIE

Organize learning around themes and projects.

> Last year we learned all about civil rights for a whole semester. We applied it to literature and history and every field, and then we went to Alabama to do the civil rights tour and go to the state house. I think that we're so interested because we learned about it and then we applied it during high school. – RACHEL W.

Model collaboration among adults.

> Our teachers work so closely together that everyone knows what the others are teaching. I picture them putting themselves in our shoes, imagining what it would be like to be one of us. What

information is being repeated that we don't need to do? What would be a really good way to integrate subjects and relate them together? If there's no communication, people feel stuck. They can't be as good as they have the potential to be. – SANA

Connect us with experts in the community.

Make opportunities for the kids you're teaching to see that what we're going to learn is going to be applied in real life. – MARQUIS

Sometimes when you're pointing out your foot in a tendu, your foot feels like a rubber band that's going to pop! If you don't get things, you break down, like, "I cannot do this, I don't want to do this anymore." But if you go see Alvin Ailey's show, you see people leaping across the stage. And they didn't start like that. They first started with the barre, like us. – MEKELZUM

If you see somebody that you really look up to, and see how successful or happy they are, you may decide to follow the path that they are in. I went to a job fair a couple of weeks ago and having these people talk about their jobs really helped me get a feel for what I was getting myself into, and how hard or easy it is to get a job. It really motivated me, meeting those professionals. – JOE

Provide opportunities for us to develop initiative and leadership.

We're going to go into the real world. We'll have to connect with many different personalities—and to relate information and skills to others in such a way that we have their respect and attention. We have to be able to take initiative, whether or not we are actually the leader of a group. Even if you're a follower, you still provide ideas, you have to be able to step out like, "This is how it needs to be done and why." You're not going to go anywhere if you don't have leadership skills, even if it's just to take control of your life and get something done. – KATHRYN

Give us choices about how to learn important subjects.

High schools should tailor their curriculum to giving students a lot
of choices. Instead of saying everyone has to take calculus, maybe
statistics is something that we find more useful. Or maybe military
history is what we're interested in, more than a general survey
course in American history. – BRIDGET

Make performance part of learning.

The moment that you have your first performance, your first showing of your art, your first reading—if people don't like it or they do
like it—you've already been pushed. There's no way out of it. And
you're not going to ignore it. – MARQUIS

Do away with class rankings.

How courses are weighted is creating a problem. If you want a
higher rank, you have to take more Advanced Placement classes.
And so in order to succeed in high school, you have to take stuff
that you're not really interested in. If someone loves dance, why
penalize them for it? – BRIDGET

Listen to the perspectives of others, including youth.

People creating the curriculum should recognize that students
aren't the same! There's a diversity in the types of learning that
we do and the types of knowledge that we acquire. – RACHEL M.

I like the idea that maybe some teacher will actually consider all of
what we've been saying and actually use it in their classroom. Even
if their students don't care, they could actually do things that make
them care. – KAREN

This Practice Project has really put everything into perspective for
me. It seems like what we do every day isn't special, but then when
we actually talk about it, it's new and interesting to somebody. It's

kind of cool that our ideas could potentially impact somebody else's life. — KATHRYN

As we concluded our work together, my young co-investigators took pleasure and pride in thinking of themselves as "experts in expertise." They now knew a great deal more about how people learn in general, and they could readily apply that understanding to their own growing mastery. Equally important, they gained pride and motivation from seeing that their new perspectives could help others—both students and teachers—get better at what they do.

At our final meeting, Bridget reflected back on the first day our group met to work together. "When you asked, 'What are you really good at?' I was struggling to find something," she said. "But now I realize I am more of an expert than I thought. I've really learned more about myself from this project, and I feel like I'm being part of a change in education, possibly. So I really hope that the work that we've done does result in some change. It would be really cool to be part of something like that."

The Practice Project

A five-day curriculum outline for secondary teachers or advisers

ESSENTIAL QUESTION: *What does it take to get really good at something?*

DAY 1

Individually or in twos or threes, students talk or write about their own experiences with getting good at something. *Examples:* basketball, running, cheerdancing, cooking, hairstyling, sewing, singing, acting, playing an instrument, stepping, drawing, slam poetry, speaking another language, building things, fixing things, and so on.

Prompts for student reflection:

- Think of something hard that you are good at doing.

- How did you first learn to do it?

- What was hardest when you first started doing it?

- What made you keep doing it even though it was hard?

- What helped you get better at it?

- Did anyone else help you with it? How?

- Describe one time when you knew you were getting better at it. How did you know?

- Once you started to get good at it, what made you want to get even better?

- Who do you trust to tell you how you're really doing? How do you know they will tell you the truth?

◆ NOTE: *To download this curriculum as a pdf, please go to www.firesinthemind.org*

DAY 2

1. Students share their reflections with the larger group.

- What was similar about your experiences of "getting good" at something?
- What was different about your experiences?
- Do you think everybody has a longing to be really good at *something*? Why or why not?

2. Students brainstorm areas in which adults out in the world get recognition because they know and/or can do something really well. *Examples:* doctors, plumbers, lawyers, media producers, police detectives, chefs, teachers, reporters, artists, auto mechanics, computer whizzes. . . .

- Do you think there is a difference between adults getting really good at what they do and *your own* experiences getting really good at something?
- Are there similarities?

3. Let's define an "expert" as someone whom people ask for help with a serious problem—something too complex to solve without specialized knowledge and experience.

- Make a list of the adults you know in your community who qualify as experts.

Name _____ Field _____

Name _____ Field _____

Name _____ Field _____

Name _____ Field _____

Name _____ Field _____

- Choose one of these adults and arrange to interview him or her in person.

Name _____

Contact information: _____

_____

_____

DAY 3

Conduct an interview with the expert you chose. Take a voice recorder so you can record the interview; if you cannot borrow a recorder, write down lots of notes. If you can bring along a camera, take photographs of the expert (at work, if possible).

Use these interview questions as a starter, then add whatever other questions you have:

- How did you first learn to do what you do?
- What was hardest when you first started doing it?
- What made you keep doing it even though it was hard?
- What helped you get better at it?
- Did anyone else help you with it? How?
- Describe one time when you knew you were getting better at it. How did you know?
- Once you started to get good at it, what made you want to get even better?
- How long did it take before people started coming to you as an "expert"?

- Who do you trust to tell you how you're really doing? How do you know they will tell you the truth?

- Write down any other questions you might want to ask:

_____

_____

_____

_____

_____

DAY 4

Transcribe (or listen again to) the recording of your interview with the expert. (If you couldn't record it, look over your written notes.) Then use this worksheet to analyze what you learned. (If you have more to say than fits here, continue writing on additional sheets of paper.)

DAY 5

As a group, compare the findings you wrote on your worksheets from Day 4.

Then summarize your conclusions about our essential question in a report from your group to your school or larger community. Below you will see one possible format for your report (or you can design your own!).

NAME OF THE EXPERT	AREA OF EXPERTISE
What (or who) got this person interested in this activity?	
What has this person found difficult (at any time) about the activity?	
What did the person do to overcome that difficulty and continue getting better?	
Who coached the person in how to improve? (teacher, employer, relative, friend, teammate, partner, other. . . ?)	
What kept the person going even when the activity got harder?	
How long did it take before people considered this person an expert?	
In what ways does this person's experience remind you of something you are learning to do?	

WHAT DOES IT TAKE TO GET REALLY GOOD AT SOMETHING?

A Report by _____ [Name of your group here]_____

To find out more about the process of developing expertise, this is what our group did:

- We interviewed _____ experts in _____ different fields. Among those fields were: [*Insert list of what your experts did.*]

- We analyzed the interviews and came to the following conclusions:

Conclusion 1._____

_____

Our evidence for Conclusion 1 included the following statements by our experts: [*Insert interview quotes that support your Conclusion 1.*]

Conclusion 2._____

_____

Our evidence for Conclusion 2 included the following statements by our experts: [*Insert interview quotes that support your Conclusion 2.*]

Conclusion 3._____

_____

Our evidence for Conclusion #3 included the following statements by our experts: [*Insert interview quotes that support your Conclusion 3.*]

Resources That Help Light Fires in the Mind

A happy corollary to our Practice Project was the chance for students and teachers to explore together the exciting work that has emerged over the past few decades, in which cognitive scientists and educators learned so much about the way mastery comes about. The materials listed here provide a variety of entry points. Some offer an introduction to the subject that might spark discussions among teachers and students; others provide structures and practices for teachers seeking ways to center classroom instruction on motivation and mastery. Some present the research itself, which is useful for teachers and students who are inspired to probe further into the development of expertise. All of these works inspired us in different ways, creating an ongoing culture among our group as we worked together to become "experts in expertise."

To join the dialogue about what you and others are reading, thinking, and doing as you work at "getting good" in and out of the classroom, please visit our web site, www.firesinthemind.org

BOOKS

Bereiter, Carl, and Marlene Scardamalia. 1993. *Surpassing Ourselves: An Inquiry into the Nature and Implications of Expertise.* Chicago: Open Court.

Bloom, Benjamin S. (ed.). 1985. *Developing Talent in Young People.* New York: Ballantine. Bloom once remarked about his landmark research in this field, "We were looking for exceptional kids and what we found were exceptional conditions"—that is, opportunity to learn, authentic tasks, and exceptionally supportive social contexts.

Blythe, Tina, and Associates. 1998. *The Teaching for Understanding Guide.* San Francisco: Jossey-Bass.

Boaler, Jo. 2008. *What's Math Got to Do with It?* New York: Viking.

Bransford, John D., Ann L. Brown, and Rodney R. Cocking (eds.). 1999. *How People Learn: Brain, Mind, Experience, and School.* Washington, DC: National Academy Press. See especially Chapter Two, "How Experts Differ from Novices," at www.nap.edu/html/ howpeople1/ch2.html.

Colvin, Geoff. 2008. *Talent Is Overrated: What Really Separates World-Class Performers from Everybody Else.* New York: Portfolio.

Cooper, Harris M. 2001. *The Battle over Homework: Common Ground for Administrators, Teachers, and Parents,* 2nd ed. Thousand Oaks, CA: Corwin Press. The author summarizes here his 1980s meta-analysis of seventeen homework studies.

Costa, Arthur L. (ed.). 2001. *Developing Minds: A Resource Book for Teaching Thinking.* Alexandria, VA: ASCD.

Coyle, Daniel. 2009. *The Talent Code.* New York: Bantam.

Csikszentmihalyi, Mihaly. 1990. *Flow: The Psychology of Optimal Experience.* New York: Harper & Row.

Csikszentmihalyi, Mihaly, and Barbara Schneider. 2000. *Becoming Adult: How Teenagers Prepare for the World of Work.* New York: Basic Books.

Csikszentmihalyi, Mihaly, Kevin Rathunde, and Samuel Whalen. 1993. *Talented Teenagers: The Roots of Success and Failure.* Cambridge, UK: Cambridge University Press.

Donovan, M. Suzanne, and John D. Bransford (eds.). 2005. *How Students Learn: History, Mathematics, and Science in the Classroom.*

Washington, DC: National Academy Press. This book describes how the three core principles of the National Research Council's 1999 report *How People Learn* (engaging resilient preconceptions, organizing knowledge around core concepts, and supporting metacognition) apply to classroom teaching and learning.

Dweck, Carol S. 2007. *Mindset: The New Psychology of Success.* New York: Random House.

Ericsson, K. Anders, Neil Charness, Paul J. Feltovich, and Robert R. Hoffman (eds.). 2006. *The Cambridge Handbook of Expertise and Expert Performance.* Cambridge, UK: Cambridge University Press. A fascinating and readable collection of important academic research in this field, from many perspectives.

Ericsson, K. Anders, Ralf Th. Krampe, and Clemens Tesch-Römer. 1993. "The Role of Deliberate Practice in the Acquisition of Expert Performance." *Psychological Review, 100*(3), 363–406. An early presentation of the "ten thousand hours" finding: expert performance generally emerges only after ten years of sustained deliberate practice in increasing increments, and research results support the key role of practice, rather than innate talent, in expert performance.

Gardner, Howard. 1991. *The Unschooled Mind: How Children Think and How Schools Should Teach.* New York: Basic Books.

Gawande, Atul. 2007. *Better: A Surgeon's Notes on Performance.* New York: Metropolitan Books. See especially "Afterword: Suggestions for Becoming a Positive Deviant," pp. 253–255.

Gladwell, Malcolm. 2008. *Outliers: The Story of Success.* New York: Little, Brown.

Harris Interactive. 2008. *MetLife Survey of the American Teacher: The Homework Experience.* New York: Metlife Foundation.

Hetland, Lois, Ellen Winner, Shirley Veenema, and Kimberly M. Sheridan. 2007. *Studio Thinking: The Real Benefits of Visual Arts Education.* New York: Teachers College Press, 2007.

Kohn, Alfie. 2000. *What to Look for in a Classroom.* San Francisco: Jossey-Bass.

Leonard, George. 1992. *Mastery: The Keys to Success and Long-Term Fulfillment.* New York: Plume.

Levine, Mel. 1992. *All Kinds of Minds.* Cambridge, MA: Educators Publishing Service.

Levine, Mel. 2003. *The Myth of Laziness.* New York: Simon & Schuster.

Lewin, Larry, and Betty Jean Shoemaker. 1998. *Great Performances: Creating Classroom-Based Assessment Tasks.* New York: Wiley.

Lieber, Carol Miller. 2009. *Getting Classroom Management Right: Guided Discipline and Personalized Support in Secondary Schools.* Cambridge, MA: Educators for Social Responsibility.

Lieber, Carol Miller. 2009. *Making Learning Real: Reaching and Engaging All Learners in Secondary Classrooms.* Cambridge, MA: Educators for Social Responsibility.

Marzano, Robert J. 1992. *A Different Kind of Classroom: Teaching with Dimensions of Learning.* Alexandria, VA: ASCD.

Marzano, Robert J. 2000. *Transforming Classroom Grading.* Alexandria, VA: ASCD.

Perkins, David. 2008. *Making Learning Whole: How Seven Principles of Teaching Can Transform Education.* San Francisco: Jossey-Bass.

Rogoff, B., and Lave, J. 1984. *Everyday Cognition: Its Development in Social Context.* Cambridge, MA: Harvard University Press.

Sennett, Richard. 2008. *The Craftsman*. New Haven, CT: Yale University Press.

Sozniak, L. A. 2003. "Developing Talent: Time, Task, and Context." In N. Colangelo and G. Davis (eds.), *Handbook of Gifted Education*, 3rd ed. Boston: Allyn & Bacon.

Stiggins, Richard J. 2007. *Student-Involved Assessment for Learning*, 5th ed. Upper Saddle River, NJ: Prentice Hall.

Tomlinson, Carol Ann. 2004. *How to Differentiate Instruction in Mixed Ability Classrooms*. Alexandria, VA: ASCD.

Vatterott, Cathy. 2009. *Rethinking Homework: Best Practices that Support Diverse Needs*. Alexandria, VA: ASCD.

Wiggins, Grant P., and Jay McTighe. 2005. *Understanding by Design*, 2nd ed. Alexandria, VA: ASCD.

Willingham, Daniel T. 2009. *Why Don't Students Like School?* San Francisco: Jossey-Bass.

Wormeli, Rick. 2006. *Fair Isn't Always Equal*. Portland, ME: Stenhouse.

Wormeli, Rick. 2007. *Differentiation: From Planning to Practice*. Portland, ME: Stenhouse.

Wolfe, Patricia. 2001. *Brain Matters: Translating Research into Classroom Practice*. Alexandria, VA: ASCD.

ARTICLES

Ohio State University. 2009. "Epidemic of Student Cheating Can Be Cured with Changes in Classroom Goals." *ScienceDaily*, http://www.sciencedaily.com /releases/2009/08/090810025249.htm. Interesting new evidence that students actually do better if the classroom focus is on mastery and not on the tests.

Wesch, M. 2008. "Anti-Teaching: Confronting the Crisis of Significance." *Education Canada*, Vol. 48, No. 2.

Washor, Elliott, Charles Mojkowski, and Loran Newsom. 2009. "At the Core of the Apple Store: Images of Next Generation Learning." Providence, RI: Big Picture Learning.

OTHER RESOURCES

Hope Study Components Checklist. 2005. From Ed Visions Schools. A method of assessing five key factors affecting student learning: their degree of choice and autonomy, support and advising, goal orientation, engagement with tasks, and level of optimism about success.

The Center on Learning, Assessment, and School Structure (CLASS), founded by Grant Wiggins, helps educators to design assessments that inform and improve performance. Contact classnj@aol.com or 609-252-1211.

Understanding by Design Exchange (www.ubdexchange.org) is a web site dedicated to the design of curriculum, assessment, and instruction that leads students to deep understanding of content. Participants can use the "backward design" template to create units and see those of others, integrate standards into unit design, and receive feedback.

Brainology®, an interactive online program designed by Carol Dweck and her colleague Lisa Sorich Blackwell to help middle and high school students develop a "growth mind-set" about learning. www.brainology.us

The *Fires in the Mind* site, www.firesinthemind.org, invites teachers, students, and communities to join our dialogue about the essential question, "What does it take to get really good at something?" Moderated by Kathleen Cushman, it also provides a place to showcase your own Practice Projects and other explorations of how youth arrive at motivation and mastery.

The Student Contributors

The 160 diverse young people who worked with me on the Practice Project came from seventeen schools in nine cities or towns around the United States. We typically met in groups, brought together sometimes in an academic class, sometimes through a school club or after-school organization, and sometimes in impromptu meetings as more adults or students heard about the work. What Kids Can Do obtained permission from all participants (and their parents or guardians, where applicable) to use their words, photographs, and first names in this book and its associated materials.

The words of ninety-two of the students with whom I worked on this project appear in *Fires in the Mind*; their names are listed here, along with their photos where available. For the many contributions of all the thoughtful students who participated, whether or not their names appear here, we owe our sincerest thanks.

Aaron S.   Aaron R.   Alex   Alexis   Amauri

Ariel B.   Ariel V.   Berenice   Bianca   Brandie

Bridget   Chanel   Chelsea   Christian   Christina

Claude   Crystal   Dan   Darrian   Deepika

Denise Q.   Denise T.   Dylan   Erika   Henry

Hunter   Iona   Jacob   Jewel   Jo'Nella

Joshua R.   Karen   Kasia   Kathryn   Kellie

Kenzie   Kirby   Kristian   Luke   Lusaida

Marquis Mekelzum Micah Mike Moira

Molly Nicholas Odell Patty Rachel C.

Rachel M. Rachel W. R.J. Rodrigo Rosalie

Ruben Samantha Shaw Tessa Tyler

Tysheena Vivian Zac

Not pictured:	Darrius	Joey H.	Josefina	Norbert
Andrew	Dina	Joey M.	Lonya	Patrick
Andris	Evan	Joshua F.	Matthew	Sana
Avelina	Evangelina	Keila	Monte	Shaquasia
Brianna	Janiy	Kelvin	Nick	Tacara
Cleven	Joe	Khoa	Ninoshka	

Acknowledgments

I must have spent ten thousand hours of deliberate practice in bringing this book to completion—and almost that many people gave generous coaching and encouragement along the way. The first spark of its idea, ignited some years ago in a conversation with Barbara Cervone, president of What Kids Can Do (WKCD), created such fires of interest in my mind that my reading shelf was soon piled high with background research. Barbara's continual intellectual companionship as well as the steadfast support of WKCD sustained me throughout the challenges of the task, for which I am deeply grateful.

MetLife Foundation's commitment to "sharing voices close to the classroom" has always included students. It has also already made possible a series of WKCD initiatives to make public the thinking of youth about their lives and learning. In supporting the Practice Project that led to *Fires in the Mind*, the Foundation saw a direct connection with its 2007 *MetLife Survey of the American Teacher: The Homework Experience.* At the press conference to launch the findings from that survey, Mary Brabeck, dean of the Steinhardt School of Culture, Education, and Human Development at New York University, spoke of her work with the American Psychological Association in that field, which greatly influenced the questions I raised with students during the Practice Project. We owe enormous thanks to MetLife Foundation for its interest, confidence, and support as students around the country investigated those questions for themselves and shared their answers with their teachers.

Those students and teachers, as well as the administrators and colleagues who supported them, played the most important role in the creation of this book as they partnered with WKCD in the Practice

Project. In its pilot stage in Chicago, funded by the McCormick-Tribune Foundation, Meg Arbeiter's eleventh graders at the Academy of Communications and Technology Charter School joined our investigation; Will Okun brought in a group of students at Westside Alternative High School; and Jessica Stephenson enlisted her ninth grade reading and writing class at Prosser Career Academy High School. In rural Maine, Joanna Payne recruited students who hoped to integrate our inquiry into their senior projects at Poland Regional High School. In San Antonio, Honor Moorman invited her students from the internship program at the International School of the Americas to join our investigation. Students at San Diego's High Tech High joined the conversation through my long and collegial friendship with Larry Rosenstock, Ben Daley, and Rob Riordan. Ted Hollister, who advises the Male Academy at Woodrow Wilson High School in Long Beach, California, facilitated several days of inquiry by the young men of color in that leadership club. With the help of Jacinda Abcarian and Erik Sakamoto, I interviewed students at Youth Radio in Oakland, California; and across the Bay at Tamalpais High School, Michelle Swanson, Susan Brashear, and Ben Cleaveland arranged for me to debrief students in the Conservatory Theatre Ensemble. In Providence, Rhode Island, Sebastian Ruth and Chloe Kline at Community MusicWorks introduced me to the young members of its String Quartet. Students also came to the Practice Project from many corners of New York City. Felice Piggott, who directs the library and media program at Young Women's Leadership School of East Harlem, brought two tenth grade classes into our inquiry. Jeanne-Marie Fraino, then principal at the Clinton School for Artists and Writers, allowed me to interview members of her eighth grade ballroom dance team. Mark Federman and Tom Mullen at East Side Community School introduced me to young skateboarders there. Lisa Nelson, principal of the Isaac Newton

Middle School for Math and Science, invited me to interview her students and graduates, particularly those in the Citizen Schools program coordinated by the extremely helpful Sharlene Jeanty. Students from the Queens High School of Teaching joined our investigation at the prompting of their tireless teacher, Ariel Nadelstern, and two assistant principals who welcomed my presence, Janine Werner and Michael Flynn. I also owe thanks to two parents, Cenceria Edwards and C. C. Blackburn, who helped me connect with their teenagers without a school as intermediary.

Throughout our Practice Project, I also gained insight by working with thoughtful educators who brought their own questions and experience to the issue of motivation and mastery. Sanda Balaban and Marina Cofield, who facilitate the Bridges for Learning Network in the Empowerment Support Organization of New York City's education department, brought me together with a group of teachers in a "Practice" study group. At the invitation of Rick Lear, who directs CES Northwest, I joined in several days of inquiry with teachers at a 2008 Summer Institute, where Jan Reeder also gave me the benefit of her many decades of experience. Many other educators individually shared their thoughts and wisdom with me at length—Ted and Nancy Sizer, Olivia Iffil-Lynch, Adria Steinberg, Elliot Washor, Liza Bearman, John Watkins, Steve Jubb, Michelle Swanson, Mary Hastings, Claire Wurzel, and Shannon O'Grady among them. Those conversations so compelled me that I began a regular "Circle of Practice" salon in my New York City home, which brought even more diverse views to inform the growing dialogue.

The student voices gathered during the Practice Project filled hundreds of transcribed pages, and without the steadfast help of Andrew Keshner, a student at Columbia's Graduate School of Journalism, I would have taken twice as long sorting their insights and stories into this book's chapters and themes. The next great challenge was mining clarity and meaning from material that, in first-person examples from kids, illustrated a daunting research base in cognitive psychology. Here I turned to my dear friend Laura Rogers, an adolescent psychologist who teaches at Tufts and Harvard and is my coauthor for *Fires in the Middle School Bathroom*. Laura's patient and incisive editorial guidance steered me through the shoals of the writing process, only adding to the endless things for which I am forever in her debt.

The same students whose voices drive this book also speak out in the accompanying audio-slideshows on which I collaborated with Justin Samaha, who also has my thanks for his close critical reading of the manuscript. Seeking images of practice, I turned to the great photographer and teacher Will Okun, whose work with youth has produced a powerful trove of captured moments, and to Patrick Hayman, who masterfully documents the work of students at High Tech High. I am sincerely grateful for their generous contributions. Finally, WKCD owes tremendous thanks to Sandra Delany, who patiently and consistently produced imaginative and elegant solutions to the graphic design dilemmas we sent her in the course of developing this book.

As always, I thank my beloved family for their loving forbearance as I put in my ten thousand hours. Connie, Celia, Montana, Eliza, Justin, Rosa, and Robert all kept me going at critical moments, and Eve, Dorothea, and Leo inspired me every day with their own delightful examples of motivation and mastery.

Kathleen Cushman
New York City
February 2010

About the Author

Kathleen Cushman writes and speaks to a national audience about the lives and learning of adolescents. A journalist and educator, over thirty-five years she has authored or coauthored twenty books, many of which resulted from her work as a reporter following national educational change efforts. In 2000 she cofounded with Barbara Cervone the nonprofit What Kids Can Do, which makes public the work and voices of youth on subjects concerning their lives and learning.

Cushman's previous books include the best-selling *Fires in the Bathroom: Advice for Teachers from High School Students,* and its sequel, *Fires in the Middle School Bathroom,* coauthored with adolescent psychologist Laura Rogers. In her book *Sent to the Principal,* teenagers speak out about school climate and culture, and in *What We Can't Tell You,* they talk candidly about their lives to parents and other close-in adults. Cushman is also author of the two-volume *First in the Family: Advice About College from First-Generation Students.* For more information, contact her through www.firesinthemind.org.

About What Kids Can Do

What Kids Can Do, Inc. (WKCD) is a national not-for-profit organization founded in 2001 for the purpose of making public the voices and views of adolescents. On its web site (www.whatkidscando.org), WKCD documents young people's lives, learning, and work, and their partnerships with adults both in and out of school. WKCD also collaborates with students around the world on books, curricula, and research to expand current views of what constitutes challenging learning and achievement. For more information, visit www.whatkidscando.org.

Support from MetLife Foundation makes it possible for teachers, parents, and students to join the dialogue begun in *Fires in the Mind* by visiting our web site and blog at www.firesinthemind.org. Moderated by author Kathleen Cushman, it welcomes all perspectives and examples that engage with this book's driving question, "What does it take to get really good at something?"

Index